Native Americans of the Northwest Coast

Veda Boyd Jones

Lucent Books, Inc.
P.O. Box 289011, San Diego, California

Titles in the Indigenous Peoples of North America Series Include:

The Apache
The Cherokee
The Cheyenne
The Iroquois
Native Americans of the Great Lakes
Native Americans of the Northeast
Native Americans of the Northwest Coast
Native Americans of the Plains
Native Americans of the Southeast
Native Americans of the Southwest
The Navajo
The Sioux

Library of Congress Cataloging-in-Publication Data

Jones, Veda Boyd.
    Native Americans of the Northwest Coast/ by Veda Boyd Jones.
        p.   cm. — (Indigenous peoples of North America)
    Includes bibliographical references and index.
    Summary: Discusses the history, daily lives, culture, religion, and conflicts of the Indians that lived on the Northwest Coast.
    ISBN 1-56006-691-1 (hardcover : alk. paper)
    1. Indians of North America—Northwest Coast of North America—Juvenile literature.   [1. Indians of North America—Northwest Coast of North America.]   I. Title. II. Series.
    E78.N78 J62   2001
    979.5'.00497—dc21   00-008053
                                                                CIP

Copyright 2001 by Lucent Books, Inc.
P.O. Box 289011, San Diego, California 92198-9011

Printed in the U.S.A.

Contents

Foreword

North America's native peoples are often relegated to history—viewed primarily as remnants of another era—or cast in the stereotypical images long found in popular entertainment and even literature. Efforts to characterize Native Americans typically result in idealized portrayals of spiritualists communing with nature or bigoted descriptions of savages incapable of living in civilized society. Lost in these unfortunate images is the rich variety of customs, beliefs, and values that comprised—and still comprise—many of North America's native populations.

The *Indigenous Peoples of North America* series strives to present a complex, realistic picture of the many and varied Native American cultures. Each book in the series offers historical perspectives as well as a view of contemporary life of individual tribes and tribes that share a common region. The series examines traditional family life, spirituality, interaction with other native and non-native peoples, warfare, and the ways the environment shaped the lives and cultures of North America's indigenous populations. Each book ends with a discussion of life today for the Native Americans of a given region or tribe.

In any discussion of the Native American experience, there are bound to be sim-

ilarities. All tribes share a past filled with unceasing white expansion and resistance that led to more than four hundred years of conflict. One U.S. administration after another pursued this goal and fought Indians who attempted to defend their homelands and ways of life. Although no war was ever formally declared, the U.S. policy of conquest precluded any chance of white and Native American peoples living together peacefully. Between 1780 and 1890, Americans killed hundreds of thousands of Indians and wiped out whole tribes.

The Indians lost the fight for their land and ways of life, though not for lack of bravery, skill, or a sense of purpose. They simply could not contend with the overwhelming numbers of whites arriving from Europe or the superior weapons they brought with them. Lack of unity also contributed to the defeat of the Native Americans. For most, tribal identity was more important than racial identity. This loyalty left the Indians at a distinct disadvantage. Whites had a strong racial identity and they fought alongside each other even when there was disagreement because they shared a racial destiny.

Although all Native Americans share this tragic history they have many distinct differences. For example, some tribes and individuals sought to cooperate almost immediately with the U.S. government while others steadfastly resisted the white presence. Life before the arrival of white settlers also varied. The nomads of the Plains developed altogether different lifestyles and customs from the fishermen of the Northwest coast.

Contemporary life is no different in this regard. Many Native Americans—forced onto reservations by the American government—struggle with poverty, poor health, and inferior schooling. But others have regained a sense of pride in themselves and their heritage, enabling them to search out new routes to self-sufficiency and prosperity.

The *Indigenous Peoples of North America* series attempts to capture the differences as well as similarities that make up the experiences of North America's native populations—both past and present. Fully documented primary and secondary source quotations enliven the text. Sidebars highlight events, personalities, and traditions. Bibliographies provide readers with ideas for further research. In all, each book in this dynamic series provides students with a wealth of information as well as launching points for further research.

A Unique Culture

It happened one night over five hundred years ago, after days of heavy rains had soaked the mountains above a village of Nootka Indians of the Makah tribe in northwest Washington.

That fateful night, people slept in the longhouses near the shoreline of the Pacific Ocean. Arranged around the huge room, which sheltered several families, were boxes of stored food, ceremonial wooden masks, fishing gear, tools, cooking boxes, hats, animal furs, woven cedar bark mats, and other items that the Indians used in their daily lives.

The Nootka longhouse was large enough to accommodate several families and their items necessary for survival.

Some totem poles were elaborate wood carvings intended to reflect the artist's idea of a supernatural being.

Above the sleeping Nootka the drenched mountainside gave way. Thousands of tons of mud slid down the incline, covering everything in its path. When the wet, heavy mud hit the Makah village, it smothered many longhouses and their occupants. It also preserved them, much as a volcanic eruption had buried the ancient city of Pompeii centuries earlier.

From an Ancient Nightmare, an Archaeologist's Dream

In 1970, heavy rains washed away part of the mud, exposing segments of the wooden houses. Archaeologists converged on the site and spent eleven years uncovering the village and sorting through thousands of artifacts.

Previously, the history of these Indians of the Pacific Northwest Coast had been documented through the eyes of white explorers and traders. Anthropologists such as Franz Boas studied the natives in the latter part of the nineteenth century, and recollections of Indians in recent times were also recorded. These formed the basis for what historians knew of the unique culture of the area. Now there were tangible items from centuries before contact with whites that added depth to the understanding of how these Indians lived.

Among the uncovered artifacts were totems, elaborate wooden carvings that resembled animals or artists' ideas of supernatural beings. One representation of a killer whale was decorated with hundreds of otter teeth. An owl's head was carved on the end of a club. Other animal designs had been carved on wooden storage boxes. This unique artwork matched the descriptions given by the first explorers who had gawked at the Indians' towering poles, elaborately carved with totems.

This art form bound the seven Indian language groups of the Pacific Northwest Coast into one culture group known as the totem pole people, named after their most spectacular artwork. Nowhere among Indian tribes in North America was the craft of ornately carved wood more developed. Many historians believe this style of art can be traced back to the Indians' roots in Asia.

Tales of ancient ancestors' encounters with creatures of the supernatural lent a mystical air to the lives of the Indians, and from these legendary events, people assumed the right to carve certain totems on their belongings. Gaining the favor of a personal guardian spirit meant that spirit's likeness could also be carved. Historians have likened these totems to heraldic crests used by European nobility. This was the Indians' way of recording their history.

An Environment Rich in Resources and Traditions

Because of the abundance of food (fish, game, and berries) in the Pacific Northwest Coast, the totem pole people developed no farming. Instead, they gathered and stored food in the summer. They devoted their winters to their art and to making items for use in their daily lives and their religious lives.

Another tie between these seven language groups was the potlatch, a ceremonial feast highlighted by the giving away of gifts to those in attendance. Prestige and rank in society mattered a great deal to these Indians because each person had a social position held by no one else. Thus it was important to have a way of proving worth, asserting privilege, and celebrating a new name and the distinction it brought. For the totem pole people, giving away

Mysterious Petroglyphs

On cliffs and boulders at nearly five hundred sites along the coast—in Alaska, British Columbia, and Washington—are images called petroglyphs. Rather primitive in form, the designs were probably cut into the rock with pointed stones. Petroglyphs represent men, animals, and mythical beasts, with occasional circles and concentric circles.

No one knows the age of these carvings. Today's Indians of the Pacific Northwest Coast claim no knowledge of them, so the oral history of these drawings has not passed down to the last few generations. Since the cliffs are exposed and no organic matter remains, carbon-14 dating techniques cannot be used. Some historians believe that most of the carvings are well over 1,000 years old. Others believe some of the drawings are as recent as 160 years old. Still others think the etchings may be older than 4,000 years.

Perhaps these were the sites of mystical experiences, or perhaps they were meant to record events. The significance of the petroglyphs remains a mystery.

one's wealth at a potlatch was a means to this end.

The unique potlatch tradition of the people of the Pacific Northwest Coast was embedded in a complex, highly structured society founded on a mystical heritage. Yet until modern times, the creators of an extraordinary original art form had a primitive gathering and storing lifestyle. This was due in large part to the rugged, weather-beaten coast on which they made their home.

Chapter 1

The People and Their Land

The totem pole Indians made their homes on a narrow strip of coastal land and the coastal islands running north from the mouth of the Columbia River in present-day Washington State. The strip extends through what is now the Canadian province of British Columbia to the Alaskan part of Yakutat Bay, a north-to-south distance of approximately fourteen hundred miles as the crow flies. But the rugged coastline with its myriad bays, fjords, islands, creeks, and inlets measures three times that distance. Hemmed in by the Coast Mountains, the thin coastal region reaches one hundred miles at its widest and narrows in places to one mile.

The Pacific Ocean pounds the shore, making navigation hazardous even today, when steel-hulled boats are powered by heavy diesel engines. When the first humans arrived on the coast of the Pacific Northwest, the only passages into the interior of the continent were narrow, deep channels cut through the mountains by rivers and streams. High tide and treacher-ous currents made these waterways difficult to maneuver.

Land and Sea: A Rough but Hospitable Environment

Indians looked up at tall mountains stretching skyward an average of 4,000 feet. Thick coniferous trees formed dark forests on these rugged mountains. Little sunlight filtered through the canopy of the trees that reached 150 feet or higher. Dank moss grew on most surfaces—rock, trees, and ground—making a hunting trip into the dim forest a slippery ordeal.

Thanks to the westerly winds, the region between the ocean and the mountains produced tremendous rainfall. In most areas there was one hundred inches of rainfall annually; in some areas, three times that amount. Fog routinely challenged the morning sun.

This rough, forbidding, wet land provided surprisingly well for its first human inhabitants, however. The warm Japan Current that flows offshore kept the climate

The rugged coastline of the Northwest Coast makes navigating the waterways a dangerous endeavor.

moderate. Temperatures dipped below freezing on only a few days each winter, and the summers were cool. The ocean and freshwater streams provided the people with fish and sea mammals. Forests yielded wildlife and berries to eat and wood for homes, clothing, fuel, and canoes.

The land did not lend itself to farming, but food was plentiful. All the original people needed was to develop the technology to gather and store it. By using objects available in their environment, the inhabitants created tools of bone and shell that allowed them to rough-hew giant red cedars into watertight canoes. Primitive sailors learned navigational skills necessary to guide the canoes

through swift waters and riptides while those in charge of the catch leaned over the edge to harpoon fish. The people developed methods to preserve their bounty and carved ornate watertight boxes in which to store their food supply. All along this unique coastland, tribes adapted to their environment.

The First People

Archaeologists agree that this land was settled at least ten thousand years ago and that the inhabitants migrated from Asia, particularly Siberia. At one time, a land bridge across the Bering Strait linked Asia with North America, allowing migrations back and forth.

Indian legends tell of people coming "out of the foam," that is, arriving from the ocean. Since such ancient tales often have a basis in fact, it may well be that people who braved sea travel followed the coast-

Beringia, the Land Bridge

Scientists believe the land bridge between Asia and Alaska in the area now called the Bering Strait was above ocean level during two prolonged periods of the last Ice Age: from thirty-six to thirty-two thousand years ago and from twenty-eight to thirteen thousand years ago. These times of massive glaciers made the ocean level over four hundred feet lower than it is today, thus allowing migrations. On this mostly marshy plain, hunters followed game through narrow, ice-free corridors into the interior of North America. During this time the coast of the Pacific Northwest was covered with ice. Around ten thousand years ago, the ice along the coast began to melt. Once the receding glaciers allowed, some Indians migrated from the interior to the coast via swift rivers. They settled in the south and moved northward. Other Indians took to the sea from Asia, followed the coast, and came ashore at the northernmost point of the Pacific Northwest Coast area and traveled south.

line of the Bering land bridge and came ashore at the foot of the mountains.

Because the beach areas were so narrow, the Indians lived in small communities scattered along the coastline. The smallest of the villages held only fifty people while the largest were home to one thousand Indians. Archaeologists suggest that in aboriginal times, that is, before the advent of European traders and a written history of these Indians, the Pacific Northwest Coast held the highest population density in North America with sixty thousand to seventy thousand people living in the narrow area, with a concentration in the south.

Ethnohistorians have grouped the people of the Pacific Northwest Coast into seven categories or "nations" based on their languages. These were not social or political territories, since early coastal inhabitants had no national consciousness. These nations were divided into some ninety tribes and further divided into clans, which consisted of people who considered themselves to be descendants of a common ancestor.

The seven nations—the Tlingit, the Tsimshian, the Haida, the Kwakiutl, the Bella Coola, the Nootka, and the Coast Salish—are further defined by the area they occupied at the time the early European explorers and traders made contact with them.

The Tlingit

The northernmost nation, which was closest to Asia geographically, was located in the southeastern Alaska panhandle. The Tlingit Indians endured the harshest winters of the totem pole

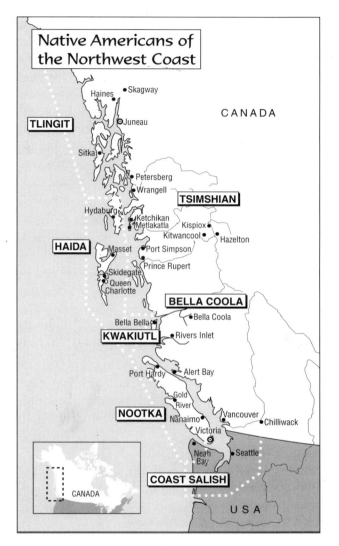

Native Americans of the Northwest Coast

Haines
Skagway

CANADA

TLINGIT

Juneau

Sitka

Petersberg
Wrangell

TSIMSHIAN

Hydaburg
Ketchikan
Metlakatla   Kispiox
Kitwancool   Hazelton

HAIDA   Masset   Port Simpson
                    Prince Rupert
Skidegate
Queen
Charlotte

BELLA COOLA

Bella Coola
Bella Bella   Rivers Inlet

KWAKIUTL

Port Hardy   Alert Bay

Gold
River
NOOTKA   Nanaimo   Vancouver
                Victoria   Chilliwack

Neah   Seattle
Bay

COAST SALISH

CANADA

USA

builders. They faced snow and ice with the same fierceness with which they faced the grizzly bear, a natural enemy they feared and respected. This fierceness was also manifested in their attitudes as warriors.

The Tlingit were the tallest of the totem pole Indians. Their average height was five feet nine inches, but some stood as tall as six feet. Unlike most Native Americans, males grew facial hair and sported beards and mustaches. The prevalent color of hair was a rich dark brown, not the black that is associated with Indians in other areas. Archaeologists interpret this characteristic as an indication of the Tlingit's close links to their Asian roots.

The Tlingit are known for their military artifacts such as helmets, weapons, and armor. They are famous for their Chilkat blankets, which are actually five-cornered robes used in ceremonial dances.

The Tsimshian and the Haida

South of the Tlingit lived the Tsimshian, whose landholdings were in what is now northern British Columbia around the Prince Rupert area. Their lands reached farther inland than any other group of totem pole builders. Many Tsimshian lived in villages along the Nass River and the Skeena River, and they controlled much of the traffic on these waterways.

Living on the Queen Charlotte Islands was the Haida nation. Several Haida tribes declared war on the Tlingit around 1700 and took two-thirds of Prince of Wales Island and several nearby islands.

The Haida were known as adventurous mariners. Shortly after their first contact

A Tlingit woman dressed in traditional clothes and accessories.

lated Puget Sound (used by the Tlingit, Tsimshian, and Haida). The Kwakiutl patrolled this inland passage, sometimes attacking voyagers and other times demanding payment for use of the waterway.

Wedged between the north and south inland expanses of the Kwakiutl was the small Bella Coola nation. This group claimed little coastline near the present-day town of Bella Bella, with most of their inland area on both sides of the Bella Coola River.

Living on the seaward side of Vancouver Island were the Nootka. Tribes in this language group also lived on the tip of northwest Washington. Location demanded they be master canoe builders, and their sturdy crafts could navigate high ocean swells. The Nootka were admired for their expertise in whale hunting.

with Europeans, they enhanced their well-built canoes by adding sails for speed.

The Kwakiutl, the Bella Coola, and the Nootka

On the northeastern coast of Vancouver Island and immediately south of the Tsimshian on the mainland lived the Kwakiutl. Their land was divided into two sections, with the small Bella Coola nation in between. The Kwakiutl controlled the northernmost entrance into heavily popu-

The Coast Salish

The southernmost nation of the totem pole builders, the Coast Salish, lived on the southeastern section of Vancouver Island and on the mainland along the coast of the Strait of Georgia and the area around Puget Sound.

This group was the smallest in stature of the Pacific Northwest Coast Indians, with an average height of five feet three inches. They also had darker complexions than the northern totem pole builders. Indians from the north frequently raided their villages for slaves.

Unique Among North American Indians

The Native Americans of the Pacific Northwest Coast developed a sophisticated material culture that was not present in any other Native American group. In the book *500 Nations,* author Alvin M. Josephy Jr. describes their material culture, which qualified these tribes for the distinction of being the wealthiest of all Indians.

Although they were maritime oriented and practiced no agriculture, they enjoyed huge harvests of fish and shellfish from the sea and rivers, as well as game and wild foods from the lush forests, which enabled them to create prosperous and complex societies. Noted as traders and raiders who plied the coastal waters in large canoes from village to village, they were among the few Indian peoples who put a value on personal wealth, which in their case included captives as well as material goods.[1]

Where there is affluence in a society, an upper class normally develops, one that many times views as inferior those with less personal wealth. Although wealth determined who was in the upper class in the totem pole Indians' world, their view of

Because of their proximity to the ocean and other waterways, the Nootka became master canoe builders.

their social position was based on family relations.

Who Was Related to Whom?

A sense of belonging to a group was paramount to these Indians, whose station in life was derived from a complicated system of kinship ties. Unraveling the social structure has proved difficult for anthropologists, who have not achieved consensus regarding this complex society. Historian Peter R. Gerber relates the formidable task of sorting through the multiple layers of relationships.

The social system of the Indians of the Northwest Coast was organized vertically as well as horizontally. Definite rules governed family relationships. Unlike our system, the most important social unit was not the nuclear family, but the so-called lineage, which included all persons related by blood who trace their descent either through the mother or the father.[2]

Through a family lineage, children received their names, family history and rights and privileges, including

Most of the Northwest Coast tribes had a complex system of determining family relationships.

The chief of the largest, wealthiest house was also recognized as the chief of the entire village.

ownership of fishing and hunting areas, berry patches, and timber regions. Northern nations—Tlingit, Tsimshian, and Haida—were matrilineal societies. Children took the mother's name and lineage connections. In the southern nations, on the other hand, descent was traced through the father's line. In the central area, the Kwakiutl chose the lineage method they wanted as children, before receiving their special ceremonial names.

Several related families lived together in households, with as many as fifty members sharing one huge house. The wealthiest of the members was the chief of the household. Usually the chief was a man, but in rare instances women served in this capacity.

One household, the wealthiest, maintained leadership in the village, and its chief became the village chief and represented the village at social engagements, an important part of the Indians' lives. However, the village chief did not have the power to rule the village, and suggestions from the community leader had to be approved by the other household chiefs.

Clan ties linked households together. Members of a clan believed they had descended from a common ancestor, a legendary personage who had associated with a spirit from the supernatural world. Such spirits came disguised as animals (such as a raven, wolf, eagle, mountain goat, or killer whale) and granted certain privileges and passed along sacred knowledge. Philip Drucker, who spent decades in the region studying the Pacific Northwest Coast Indians, states that clan members were regarded as close relatives.

> [T]hey jointly owned lands of economic importance, house and camp sites, and a host of privileges—ceremonial names or titles for chiefs and their lesser brethren, house names, ritual performances, songs and the like. Perhaps most important were the crests, the animal or monster figures associated with each clan.[3]

Membership in a given clan allowed a person to use that clan's totem as an emblem of the alliance. Clan members would carve, paint, or weave this totem and other crests on their property, including houses, poles, baskets, wooden boxes, fishing hooks, weapons, ladles, ornaments, canoes, and clothing. They even used totem images as designs for tattoos.

The Social Hierarchy: Nobles and Commoners

Social status was very important to the totem pole Indians, since a person's position in society was based on wealth and inherited privilege. Nobles, who formed the upper level of the social hierarchy, were influential people perceived as having wisdom as well as wealth. The wealthiest of these nobles was the chief. Nobles owned more food, blankets, and canoes than others in their villages, and they rarely performed menial tasks like carrying water or fetching firewood. They wore finer clothes than other tribe members. Their jewelry, made of wood, bone, or shells, was also larger and heavier than others could afford.

Commoners, who formed the middle class of society, were related to the chief, but often the connection was distant. In some cases, however, the connection was close, since the youngest sibling in a noble family would have commoner status if elder brothers had inherited all the high ranks available in that village. Certain professions, such as canoe building and wood carving, were reserved for commoners. Master craftsmen were treated with respect, however, and the elevated social status they enjoyed was a sign of social stratification among members of a single class.

In the north the division between nobles and commoners was rather distinct. The Tlingit, the northernmost totem pole group, called those of high rank "good," while they called commoners "poor children" or "just anything." In the southern areas, wealth had more to do with the division of class than inherited privileges. Here the line between nobles and commoners was not so finely drawn. It was possible for a commoner to amass wealth

A Mark of Distinction

A sign of nobility in a woman was a flat, backward-sloping forehead. To achieve this mark of beauty and social rank, an infant girl was strapped in a cradleboard with a cedar-bark pad securely tied across her forehead. Over several months the baby's head was elongated by the pressure from the pad. Apparently this procedure did not cause pain or in any way affect mental processes.

The resulting profile of a noble totem pole Indian woman is reminiscent of silhouettes of Egyptian women with their upward and backward sloping hairstyles. Even today's wedge haircut mimics this noble look.

A sloping forehead was considered a sign of beauty and nobility.

and claim noble status, and it was also possible for a noble to become impoverished and move downward on the social ladder.

Historian Philip Drucker comments on the social order:

Consequently, the two principles of societal organization—social rank and kinship—did not conflict, but modified each other. While the concept of hereditary rank was of great importance, it did not produce a sharply defined class or caste of aristocrats who exploited and oppressed those of lowly birth, as has occurred in other areas where similar social concepts have developed. The North Pacific Coast chief or noble did not grind the faces of the lowborn of his social unit, because they were not his subjects or his serfs: they were his kinsmen, and therefore entitled to special consideration.[4]

The Lowest of the Low: Slaves

The lowest sector of society was the slave class, who were not viewed as real people but as material possessions. These were men, women, and children who had been abducted from other villages, usually far down the coast. When nobles or commoners were kidnapped during a raid on a nearby village, their relatives could pay a ransom for them. When the raiders came from far down the coast, however, the captives' chances of being ransomed were slim.

Although slaves worked hard, generally they were well treated because they were regarded as belongings. They were a sign of wealth for the slave owner, who might own only one or fifty or more slaves. A firsthand description of slave life comes from John Jewitt, an English sailor who was captured by the Nootka in the early 1800s:

> They reside in the same house, forming as it were a part of the family, are usually kindly treated, eat of the same food, and live as well as their masters. [They] are compelled however at times to labour severely, as not only all the menial offices are performed by them, such as bringing water, cutting wood, and a variety of others, but they are obliged to make the canoes, to assist in building and repairing the houses, to supply their masters with fish, and to attend them to war and to fight for them.[5]

Slaves were allowed to marry and have a family life of their own. However, children of a marriage were also slaves and could be traded, sold, or given away as gifts. Occasionally slaves were themselves owners of slaves.

Valued as they were as symbols of wealth, slaves nonetheless had reason to fear for their lives. They were disposable. If a child of a nobleman died, one or two slave women might be killed to care for the child in the afterlife. The bereaved father

could always buy more slaves. Slaves who became ill would be nursed back to health if they were well liked and performing useful work in the household. But those who were old or infirm might be left in the woods to die.

Outside the Hierarchy: Shamans

A nonclass, those not subject to chiefs or involved in the day-to-day need to accu-

Slave Raids

Slaves were a sign of great wealth, since owning them showed that the master was not only supporting himself and his family but could afford to feed extra mouths. Warriors, many times the younger sons of chiefs, raided villages up and down the coast to obtain slaves. After beaching their canoes, warriors would steal into a village at dawn, surprising the people in the houses closest to the landing site. It was not uncommon for warriors to kill the men in the house, since they could be expected to cause trouble by trying to escape. Young women and children were herded into the canoe and taken back to the warriors' village. Some slaves were ransomed, others were traded for items such as blankets or sea otter pelts, and still others were kept as servants. In all these ways, slaves contributed to the wealth and prestige of their owners.

The shaman, or medicine man, was a highly influential part of the villagers' lives.

mulate wealth, were shamans, the medicine men of the tribes. These respected sages learned the healing power of herbs and had immense influence over every detail of the villagers' lives. They lived apart from the other tribe members, but of necessity followed the patterns of life imposed by the cyclic existence of the coastal people.

Seasonal Cycles

Life for the Indians fell into two distinct areas governed by the seasons. During the spring and summer the Indians camped inland on the rivers and creeks as they gathered food. The dark, rainy months of winter found them in their small villages along the coast. Year after year as the Indians of the Pacific Northwest Coast moved back and forth, their lives took on a pattern, and they developed a unique culture not shared by any other Indian group.

Chapter 2

Summer Harvest

The Indians of the Pacific Northwest Coast regulated their lives by the seasons. In the early spring and summer, they moved from their permanent homes along the coast to areas inland, gathering food that would last through the winter months. Although berries were picked and forest animals were hunted during this period to

Each year, salmon swim upstream to spawn. This event was greeted with rejoicing by the various tribes because of how important salmon were to their survival.

add to the pantry, fishing provided the most bounty.

Swarms of Candlefish

The earliest gathering period began along the big rivers in the land of the Tsimshian. Usually in March, slender eulachon (about six inches long) headed up the Nass River before it was completely clear of ice. These oily fish were called savior fish by the Tsimshian because they were so important to their daily existence. Along the coast the eulachon were also known as candlefish because they could be burnt like a candle when they were dried. Whether used as a greasy seasoning or to light a dark night, eulachon were the Tsimshian's biggest trade commodity.

The Salmon Run

Although the coastal Indians were dependent on all types of fish for their food, none was as important as the salmon. Five species of Pacific salmon (chinook, coho, sockeye, pink, and chum) swam up the rivers to spawn in the areas where they were born. The chinook began the journey to fresh water in May, and the chum left the ocean to lay their eggs in the rivers in September. Each species was greeted with great rejoicing by the Indians, who performed a special ceremony to welcome it.

The Indians of the Pacific Northwest Coast believed the salmon were people who lived in an undersea world. Once a year they transformed themselves into fish to provide food for the natives. If the

Candlefish Oil

The trading crop of the Tsimshian was the rich oil of the slender eulachon, which were caught in enormous numbers. Canoe loads of these candlefish were thrown into large, covered pits and left to decompose. Once this process had reached a certain point, the foul-smelling remains were scooped into wooden boxes. In the standard method of cooking, water was added to the boxes and brought to a boil by adding fire-heated stones. Oil was skimmed off the top of the boiling water. As the oil cooled, it thickened. The stench accompanying this method of rendering grease was powerful, but to the Tsimshian it was merely a reminder of the great wealth the fish brought them.

salmon were badly treated, they might not return again, so the first salmon rites were carefully observed to show respect for the salmon-people's sacrifice.

After the first salmon was caught, the village celebrated the bounty they were about to receive. During the entire ceremony, the head of the fish was kept pointing upstream to encourage others to follow it. The fish was cleaned and the skeleton returned to the water so that the salmon-person could rejuvenate herself and return again the following year. After the salmon had been sprinkled with eagle down, cooked, and welcomed with speeches, each person ate a small piece of the fish. Some tribes observed a few days of welcome before families took to the streams and rivers. Others immediately began packing for the journey to fish camps on the rivers, which through heredity belonged to their household or clan.

Summer Homes

In the summer, boys, girls, men, and women carried empty storage boxes to canoes. Some men pried planks off their winter homes to use in the summer locations. Cedar-bark mats were stowed on board. Of course, fishing equipment and the sharp shell knives for filleting the fish were necessities. Once the canoes were loaded, family groups headed upriver.

In some of the more permanent fish camps, Indians had built standing log frameworks for houses. Men attached the planks they had taken from their coastal homes and so were safe and dry from the summer rains. Other families built lodgings out of brush along the riverbank. Still others built a temporary framework out of poles and covered it with tightly woven mats. All the structures were small, only allowing room for the family to lie down at night and for storing the food they would take back to their winter quarters.

Rarely did a family stay in one location the entire summer. Different types of salmon made their annual journeys at different times, and people moved from stream to stream accordingly. They also returned to their winter homes between

Packing for the Trip

Although the Indians needed many boxes and baskets in which to store their food harvest, they had no need of suitcases for their summer trips to fish camps and berry patches. Except for the northern areas where it was cooler, men and children wore no clothing. Women wore cedar-bark aprons or skirts. On rainy days all would don closely woven cedar-bark capes which shed water. A hat completed their rain gear. No one wore footwear because moccasins would merely get wet and soggy.

foraging trips inland to store their harvest and fetch more empty storage boxes and baskets.

Catching the Salmon

Once the camps were in order, fishing began. Individual fishermen continued the ritual of thanking the salmon for giving its body for food. A typical prayer at a fish camp, offered to the spirit of a fish before returning its skeleton to the water, was recorded by anthropologist Franz Boas, who was one of the first scholars to study the culture firsthand.

> Welcome, Swimmer. I thank you, because I am still alive at this season when you come back to our good place; for the reason why you come

is that we may play together with my fishing tackle, Swimmer. Now, go home and tell your friends that you had good luck on account of your coming here and that they shall come with their wealth bringer, that I may get some of your wealth, Swimmer, friend, Supernatural one.[6]

The salmon were so thick in the river, legend says a person could walk across the river on their backs. With such a plentiful supply, the Indians' rather primitive tools were sufficient to kill the salmon. Indeed, they had studied the fish and its migration patterns, and through experience had learned the best way to catch them. One white surveyor who traveled widely along the coast in the 1800s

remarked, "There is little in the art of fishing we can teach these Indians."[7]

Methods of catching salmon varied from stream to river as width, depth, swiftness of current, and species of salmon dictated. The easiest way to catch the spawning fish proved to be by building weirs across rivers. A weir is a fence with one or more funnel-shaped openings just large enough for the fish to enter as they swim upstream. When salmon entered a funnel, encountered the barricade, and tried to escape, they were drawn into long, narrow traps. Because of the density of the fish in the traps, men could easily spear them or pull them out with cedar bark nets and into their canoes. Another method was

The abundance of salmon in the rivers guaranteed that many would be caught by simply lowering a net.

to build catwalks above the weirs and use spears or nets for the fish.

Catching a winter's supply of salmon was not difficult, but it was work. Successful fishing required more perseverance than skill. The more industrious the worker, the larger the catch. Historian Philip Drucker describes a typical workday at a Tsimshian fish camp:

Men and older boys tended the traps or harpooned or dip-netted, then carried the fish back to camp. The womenfolk hunkered over their cutting boards, sliming and gutting the fish, then slicing them thin with mussel-shell blades. The fish were spread with wooden skewers to dry. There was wood to get—spruce and fir knots to keep the fires going, and half-rotten alder to make the smoke that gave the fish a pleasant flavor. Fish were smoked in large plank structures. Men helped their wives rustle wood, and gave them a hand at turning over yesterday's catch, moving day-before-yesterday's fish higher on the drying racks, and hanging up the fish just prepared. There were skewers to be prepared for next day, a damaged harpoon tip to be repaired, or other chores to tend to. The period of salmon fishing was a busy season, with no time for play.[8]

At some fish camps, the air was dry enough for the fish to dry in the sun's warmth. In damp areas, smoking was necessary to preserve the catch. When the salmon were totally dried so that they would not mold, they were placed in watertight boxes made especially for fish storage.

Picking Berries

Occasionally the women would take a few hours from working the salmon to pick berries in

Salmon Traps

LATTICE WEIR
Submerged at Flood Tide

Ebb Tide

COVE
Dry at Ebb Tide

Current

Current

After being caught, salmon was often smoked in order to preserve it for eating throughout the winter.

nearby patches that belonged to their household or clan. But only after the salmon run was over did berry picking begin in earnest. Once again the family would move, building temporary shelters near berry patches, the rights to which were passed down from generation to generation within a specific group. Abundant berry patches included salalberries, huckleberries, cranberries, salmonberries, strawberries, and soapberries. The Indians ate their fill of the berries, the only sweet-tasting substance in their diets. Most of the berries were preserved in fish oil for what the people considered to be a tasty treat during the winter months. A few were squished into juice and preserved in that manner. Salalberries were cooked into a thick pulp and sun-dried in small cakes.

Gathering Vegetables

Although the coastal Indians were not agrarian, they gathered what edible vegetables they could find. The roots of clover and certain ferns were dried. Thistles were pounded into a powder to make a flourlike substance. When mixed with water and baked, it made hard loaves that preserved well.

The inner bark of the hemlock made an interesting side dish. Wild onions or bulbs

To supplement their diets, the Indians of the Northwest Coast would gather wild rice and whatever other edible vegetables they could find.

of the camas plant added variety to a menu that consisted mainly of fish. The Indians' diet also included game, however, and the men took great pride in their ability to hunt.

Hunting for Game

From boyhood, future hunters were taught to shoot their arrows straight, throw spears, and set snares and deadfall traps. Game animals were hunted not only for their meat, but also for their skins and fur, which were used for clothing and as trading commodities. Plenty of game was available in the forests and near the streams: fox, timber wolf, beaver, ermine, marten, mink, lynx, black and grizzly bears, deer, bighorn sheep, and mountain goats. Of course, different animals were available in different areas.

Special hunting dogs were used by many tribes. The Tlingit bred a terrier-like dog especially for bear hunting. When training the pup, the Indians would cut the pup's nose and rub it with the entrails or fur of a bear. Despite this seemingly harsh treatment, a special relationship usually developed between a hunter and his dog. An early nineteenth-century visitor to a Tlingit village remarked, "there was surely a dog apiece to every member of the community, and then, perhaps, some to spare."[9]

Occasionally men enlisted the help of others in the household to flush out game. Women and children would make a huge circle around the area where hunters suspected deer were hiding. Once given a signal, they would yell and clap and stomp, making as much noise as they could. Startled deer would run right into the open where hunters with bows and arrows waited. The so-called surround method of hunting was used by Native American tribes all over the continent. More specialized techniques, unique to the Pacific Northwest Coast tribes, were required to catch the large sea mammals on which the people depended for food and oil.

Sea Hunting, Active and Passive

Sea animals, such as seals, sea lions, sea otters, and porpoises followed the schools of fish toward the rivers. Hunters jumped in their sleek canoes to sneak up quietly on the creatures and prove their skill in outwitting the powerful swimmers. With their clubs held high, the hunters waited for their opportunity and then pounded on the animals. Like other game, these animals were used for their fur and meat. Sea lions were especially sought for their tasty meat and their intestines, which were emptied of waste, then shaped into watertight containers, harpoon floats, or bowstrings.

Hunters also went to sea to find their prey. Such a quest was not undertaken lightly. The book *Keepers of the Totem* describes the ritual of one hunter:

One renowned Nootka seal hunter prepared for an expedition by bathing in the ocean for four nights during the waxing moon [the period when the moon's

The hunting of seals, sea lions, and other sea animals provided much-needed oil and another source of food.

lighted portion is increasing]. He began each night's ritual by rubbing himself with a particular seaweed. Next, he prayed in a loud voice, then slipped into the water and—to encourage his future quarry not to dive—swam with his head raised high for as long as he could bear the cold. He repeated the procedure 10 times each night.[10]

The biggest sea mammal, the whale, was the most highly prized specimen of the ocean's bounty. Besides the large amount of fresh meat it provided the Indians, its blubber provided whale oil, a precious commodity.

Each summer dead whales washed ashore during storms. The Indians did not believe these were merely random acts of the sea giving up her dead. Success in enticing a dead whale to a particular village's shore was attributed to whale fishermen believed to have ritual powers. The rituals were kept secret, but many times involved shrines of skulls and corpses of the whaler's ancestors. These whalers were treated with the same high regard as those who risked their lives in the ocean on a whale hunt. After all, the result was the same: whale oil and food for the entire village.

The Nootka on the seaward side of Vancouver Island were unsurpassed in their whale-fishing expertise. They combined years of experience and knowledge with spiritual help and challenged the sea for its "noble ladies." This term of respect was applied to whales, which no fisherman could call by name during the hunt for fear of bringing bad luck.

Preparing for a Whale Hunt

Preparing for a whale hunt took time and dedication. Each hunter had his own ritual, which might include painting his face, swimming counterclockwise in fresh water,

A Whaling Harpoon

Fishing equipment had to be in the best condition. In *Cultures of the North Pacific Coast,* historian Philip Drucker describes the ingenious device used for whale hunting.

"The Nootkan whaling harpoon, complete with shaft, foreshaft, and head, was nearly twenty feet long. The heavy seasoned yew shaft was three or four inches in diameter, and tapered to its ends. It was made in three sections so skillfully joined that it appeared to be a single flawless piece of wood. Two pieces of elkhorn formed a slot for a blade of giant mussel shell, which was held in place with a coating of spruce gum. The two pieces of elkhorn and shell were lashed together, the lashing also forming a lanyard with an eye splice for the main line. When the shell broke on a strike, as often happened, the elkhorn pieces remained as barbs."

or making the blowing sound of a whale. In some tribes only the chief could drive the harpoon. In other tribes, a man trained in the art of harpooning from the time he was a young boy was in charge of the whale hunt.

The wife of the main whaler was also important in the hunt. While the hunters were out in their canoes, she remained in camp, as quiet and motionless as possible. She represented the whale and controlled its movements. If she remained still, the whale would be docile. Any sudden movement on her part would mean the whale could dive or be hard to approach.

A normal whaling party consisted of three canoes, which would leave shore at dawn. The hunters never knew how long they might be gone. If they were extraordinarily lucky, they would return towing a whale by evening. Sometimes several days passed before they would sight a whale and successfully bring it ashore. Other times a whaling party would be lost at sea. Always, however, the departure of the whaling canoes was a major event for the village.

The Excitement of the Chase

When a whale was sighted, the chief's canoe pulled alongside the huge quarry. The paddlers had to be swift and quiet so that the whale would not dive. They positioned

A chief readies his harpoon and other supplies in preparation for an upcoming whale hunt.

the canoe close to the whale's side. The chief or the harpooner stood up, holding the heavy harpoon. At the exact moment, he drove the harpoon into the whale just behind the flipper.

Hunters furiously paddled the boat out of harm's way as the great animal lunged forward and sounded, carrying the harpoon line of twisted cedar and four sealskin floats underwater. The shaft of the harpoon broke off as intended and floated to the surface. The smallest of the three canoes recovered it and headed back to shore to notify the others of a successful strike.

When the whale surfaced, the chief in one canoe and a relative of his, usually a younger brother, would take turns striking it with additional harpoons tied to float lines. The chief would speak to the dying whale, asking it to swim to shore: "Our people will welcome you. We will sing and dance and decorate your great body with feathers."[11]

The Indians believed that if all the hunters had successfully carried out their training rituals before the hunt, the whale would turn toward shore and let itself be killed in front of the villagers. Any other outcome was interpreted as a sign that someone had not been faithful in his training. If the whale swam out to sea before she was too exhausted to swim anymore, hunters had to chase her again to be able to wing the killing lance to the heart. Then the tedious job of towing the whale to shore would begin.

When the whaling vessels were sighted by those on shore, additional canoes were paddled out to help with the towing. When the whale was beached, the chief's wife would be waiting to greet the whale with a cup of fresh water and eagle down. Historian Philip Drucker reconstructs a typical speech: "Oh, noble lady, welcome to our village. We have been waiting long for you to honor us with your visit. I bring you sweet water and sacred food."[12]

The ceremony continued as the chief gave a speech and received the first cut of blubber from the whale. Visiting chiefs of

Fishing for Dentalia

The long white dentalia shells so valued by the Indians were normally found in deep water, where they could not be harvested by primitive means. But because of ocean currents, dentalia beds are found in a few places at moderate depths on the seaward side of Vancouver Island.

Fishing over these dentalia beds required a special long tool that could reach to the ocean floor. The fishing contraption at one end of a long pole was made of hardwood splints and resembled a Halloween witch's broom. Fitted above the broom "bristles" was a stone-weighted board with a hole in the middle that allowed it to slide down the pole. Additional poles were lashed to the contraption with nettle-fiber cordage to reach the required depth. When the fisherman jabbed his pole into the bed, flattening the splints, the board would slide down and force the splints close together. The fisherman, upon pulling up the pole, hoped to find several shells pinched between the splints. The work was time consuming, but the beds were rich, and the result was worth the effort. The Nootka dentalia fishermen cleaned their catch, sorted them into three sizes (long, short, and in-between), and traded them to neighbors.

nearby villages would also receive large slabs. Other nobles received strips of blubber, and then those who had participated in the hunt received blubber. At the end of the feast, the chiefs and whale hunters would leave the rest for the commoners, who would strip the carcass before sundown.

Mollusk Collecting: From Dentalia to Clams

Besides being masters of whaling, the Nootka were also the group primarily responsible for harvesting dentalia—tiny, slender, tapered white mollusks, valued for their shells. Dentalia beds are located in moderately deep water off the coast of Vancouver Island. These rare shells were used as a special decoration and were the closest equivalent to money the prehistoric Indians had. Although dead shells washed ashore all along the coast, they lacked luster and thus were not a trade commodity like the ones taken alive from the Nootka beds.

All along the coast and nearly any time of year, clams, mussels, and other ordinary mollusks could be collected. At low tide, even children could poke around with a sharp-pointed stick, dig out the shellfish, and throw them in a basket. Near each village a pile of shells attested to the abundance of shellfish as a fresh component of the Indians' diet.

Trading the Summer Harvest

When the generous summer gathering time spilled over into fall, and families had returned to their houses along the coast with their bounty of fish, berries, vegetables, and game preserved and stored, the excess was traded. Up and down the coast, Indians took to canoes with their wares.

From the north the Tsimshian brought the valued candlefish oil and also traded it to interior Indians on what became known as grease trails because of the nature of their commodity. The Nootka offered dentalia shells, whale oil, and slaves. The Tlingit traveled south with their Chilkat blankets. The Haida were known for their well-crafted canoes. The Coast Salish traded baskets and blankets woven from mountain goat hair and dog hair.

With the busy gathering and trading season finished, the Indians settled down for the winter season in their coastal villages.

Chapter 3

Life in Winter

During the winter months, the totem pole Indians lived in villages along the shores of sheltered saltwater bays or along river outlets. Villages ranged in population from fifty people to around one thousand. Houses were arranged in a long row parallel to the shoreline and built one hundred feet or more above high tide line. Other structures—sweat houses, smokehouses, storage sheds, and seclusion huts—were usually behind the main houses. Larger villages had two rows of houses some twenty feet apart and could consist of thirty or more houses. The more populated villages might stretch as much as a mile long.

A house was owned by the house chief, but members of the household had a vested interest in the house. The property from the house to the shoreline was used to store canoes and as a front yard. Spaces between houses were treated much as modern alleys, and were shared between the two neighboring houses.

Indian villages varied in size and were usually built along the shores of bays or rivers.

House Design

The Indians of the Pacific Northwest Coast were engineers of sorts. Rather than

The Indians of the Northwest Coast used the abundant wood that was available to build their longhouses.

digging mud and shaping it into bricks like the southwestern Indians, they used nature's abundance in their environment as raw material for their homes. The western red cedar was known as the "giant tree of life." It could grow to an amazing height of 231 feet with a diameter of 17 feet, and it could live up to one thousand years. By using only an ax, a wedge, and an adze (a tool like an ax but with an arching blade at right angles to the handle), the Indians could split trees into usable shapes. From this lumber, they built huge homes which the Salish called a "longhouse" and which the more northern groups called a "big house."

Larger homes could run 160 feet long by 40 feet wide. In the southern area, the Salish sometimes built houses end to end so that doorways opened up between the houses and structures stretched 650 feet long. But normal homes formed a rectangle of 20 or more feet wide by 50 to 100 feet long, with those in the south usually larger than those in the north.

House Building

Building a new house or rebuilding an existing home was a goal of each chief, for a leader's dwelling was a measure of his importance and wealth. If he were unable to achieve this goal, then his successor would feel a solemn obligation to carry out the plan.

Four huge corner posts were lifted into place using a post-and-tackle system. Other centrally located roof-support posts and framing posts were erected in the same way. Carefully split planks formed the sides and were fitted on the frame either vertically or horizontally, then secured with wooden pegs or tied with woven cedar rope. These side boards could be easily removed for emergency exits.

The front of a rich man's house might be whitewashed with lime and painted with a huge symbol of the owner's lineage—perhaps a killer whale or a beaver. Other homes might have a plain front with only a house pole as decoration. The small opening through this pole provided the only entry into the rectangular house. On the pole were carved the totems of the clan and the family lineage.

John Jewitt, the Boston seaman who was captured by the Nootka, admired the people's building acumen and wrote of the way the houses were roofed:

[T]he top is covered with planks of eight feet broad, which form a kind of coving projecting so far over the ends of the planks that form the roof, as completely to exclude the rain. On these they lay large stones to prevent their being displaced by the wind. The ends of the planks are not secured to the beams on which they are laid by any fastening, so that in a high storm, I have often known all the men obliged to turn out and go upon the

roof to prevent them from being blown off, carrying large stones and pieces of rock with them to secure the boards; always stripping themselves naked on these occasions, whatever may be the severity of the weather, to prevent their garments from being wet and muddied, as these storms are al-

Supernatural Beings: Raven, the Trickster

In the beginning, according to time-honored myths of the totem pole tribes, Animal People roamed the earth. These supernatural creatures, which lived and acted like humans, had the ability to change back and forth from animal form to human form. Some were good, some were evil, and some were monsters.

One myth recounts the story of Raven, the trickster. Although he was rather selfish, the things he did to satisfy his own desires also helped people. He stole a box from the sky chief and opened it, allowing the sun to escape, and thus brought light to the world. He also took fresh water from another chief but spilled some drops, which created the rivers and lakes. From yet another chief, he stole fire. He tricked another chief into making the eulachon run into the rivers from the ocean, which allowed the Indians to obtain these candlefish.

family might have its own fire pit. Because the fires were not well vented, a haze hung over the dark interior of the large houses.

Inside the Houses

Historian Joseph H. Wherry drew upon the journals of early European explorers for his description of the enclosed spaces.

Entering the typical dwelling through the front . . . the visitor found himself on a floor of planks laid upon leveled ground. Running lengthwise, and occupying a fourth to a third of the interior width, was the fire and cooking area a foot or so lower, giving the interior something of a covered courtyard look. On all four sides, integral with and on the same level as the entry, was a ramp or "grade" similarly planked. In extremely large houses there was often an additional level or two several feet wide; these served as convenient storage places for the ever-present carved wooden boxes of all sizes that housed all sorts of personal belongings, blankets, and other valuables. Occasionally, where interior horizontal beams were needed, these were elaborately carved.[14]

At the end opposite the doorway resided the chief of the household and his family.

The entrances to homes were often decorated with house poles showing the family's lineage.

most always accompanied by heavy rains. . . . [The houses] are wholly without a chimney, nor is there any opening left in the roof, but whenever a fire is made, the plank immediately over it is thrust aside, by means of a pole, to give vent to the smoke.[13]

In smaller homes, there might be only one central fireplace used by all the inhabitants for cooking, but in other homes each

Along the sides on the raised platforms were cubicles, divided by screens or piles of cedar boxes. These cubicles served as the bedrooms for other family units who lived in the house, and the floors were covered with woven cedar-bark sleeping mats. The rank of the members determined how close their cubicle was to the chief's. In decreasing rank, the families' cubicles encircled the perimeter. Those of the lowest rank or slaves slept nearest the door.

John Jewitt noted the furnishings in the interior of a Nootka dwelling as

> boxes, in which they put their clothes, furs, and such things as they hold most valuable; tubs for keeping their provisions of spawn and blubber in; trays from which they eat; baskets for their dried fish and other

purposes; and bags made of bark matting, of which they also make their beds.[15]

A Time of Maintenance

Repairs on the home—replacing plank walls, flooring, and roofing—were carried out during the winter months, as the rainy season permitted. Mats, which hung on the interior walls to keep out the wind, were mended. Also at this time, more elaborate carvings were done on interior posts. The more ornate the interior, the more prestige belonged to the household chief.

Winter was also the time for repairing cooking boxes. Because the Indians of the Pacific Northwest Coast did not make pottery, they had no method of placing cooking utensils on a fire. Instead, they heated

Watertight Wooden Boxes

Native Americans perfected a design for watertight boxes whose sides were formed from one piece of wood. After cutting a cedar board to an even thickness, a carpenter would cut three transverse grooves (kerfs) almost through the board. These grooves had to be perfectly square and spaced exactly in the right spots so that the board could be folded on itself to form tight seals. The board was steamed over hot stones in a pit until the kerf was pliable and could be bent at a right angle. The ends of the board were beveled for a tight fit and sewn together

through drilled holes or pegged with wooden pieces. The bottom of the box was measured to fit the folded sides and formed a mortise joint held in place by wooden pegs driven into drilled holes. Several types of covers were made: one was a thick board hollowed out to fit exactly over the box; another was a board grooved like the bottom board; and yet another was a shorter-sided inverted box. All were carved with crests belonging to the clan or household or with animal crests, or other symbols. Whale oil and eulachon oil were stored in these boxes.

beach cobblestones in the fire until they were glowing hot, then placed them in wooden boxes which held soup or water for boiling fish and game. Cooking boxes were made in an intricate manner of notching and bending wood for sealed, watertight joints.

Winter Industries

Craftsmen made new wooden storage boxes during dismal winter days. The wooden objects were sanded with dogfish skin, polished, and elaborately carved with totems of the family. Corners of storage boxes were square and neatly formed, and all containers were symmetrical.

Tools were fashioned on rainy winter days. A hunter could easily wield a solid branch to kill a sea lion, but the totem pole Indians preferred not to use plain, unembellished clubs. With pride, they carved rough sticks into polished weapons, many times covering them with low-relief designs.

Women spent the winter months weaving blankets, capes, hats, and baskets. They combined flexible roots of spruce, inner bark of cedars, mountain goat wool, dog wool, and down from ducks and other birds as their thread. Their goal was to make waterproof clothing and watertight containers. Some of the baskets were so tightly woven, they were used for cooking by the hot-stone boiling method.

Winter Hunting and Gathering

The winter food supply of dried fish was supplemented by fresh game caught in the nearby forests. Hunting parties relied on the same hunting techniques they used in summer, and they regularly checked their traps and snares.

Mollusks were always available in tide pools and bays and provided another variation in the Indians' winter diet. Not only did the meat provide a tasty treat, but the mollusks' shells were used for decoration for inlay work, ornaments, and jewelry, and as household tools. Special loosely woven baskets were made for collecting clams. Sand and pebbles could be washed out by merely dipping the basket in clear water. So abundant were clams that ancient sites of Indian villages can still be located by huge piles of clam shells called middens.

Just as understandable as the practice of accumulating clamshells was the need for families to keep busy during the long nights of winter, when outdoor activities were impractical.

Long Winter Nights

To pass a cool, rainy night, the Indians played games. A favorite was clowning to make another player laugh. Coordinating movements with closed eyes was another contest among players.

The most popular entertainment was storytelling. Grandfathers gathered children around the fire and told myths or hero tales. Stories told how the lakes were formed and why the sun gave light. Many stories featured the trickster, Raven, while others starred Stone-Ribs, a character made mostly of stone and therefore practically

Ornaments

Both sexes wore ornaments in the form of shell necklaces, earrings, or nose rings. Only women wore labrets, elliptical objects of bone or wood, grooved like a pulley and worn in a slit cut in their lower lips. A noble girl would wear a small labret. As she grew, the size of her labret would increase. An elderly woman might wear a labret nearly three inches in length.

Tattoos were also popular among Native Americans. Among the northern nations, boys and girls of noble status might be decorated with many crest designs. Fewer tattoos were used in the south.

Both men and women wore decorative nose rings (pictured), necklaces, and earrings.

invincible. Some stories belonged to a certain family lineage, while others belonged to the community as a whole.

Building a Totem Pole

While oral stories of their heritage drew a household together, a more permanent history of its legends, myths, genealogy, and events of importance was created in the form of a totem pole. The animals associated with an ancestor's encounter with the spirit world were carved as crests or totems on a giant cedar log. In addition to the animal images, a totem pole could feature carvings representing human beings.

There were various types of totem poles, some universally used, others characteristic of a particular area. Memorial poles were the most important and were usually commissioned by the person who assumed the title and privileges of a deceased person. They were stand-alone units that served only to commemorate the dead. House posts, on the other hand, had two purposes: to hold up the sides and roof of the house and to serve as decoration. House front or portal poles served as the entrance to the house and as a status symbol by showing inherited and acquired crests. They varied from twenty-five to fifty feet tall, with the portal opening usually three feet high. Welcoming poles or waterfront owner poles, which declared ownership of a beach, were seldom seen in the north. Northern groups were distinguished by their use of grave totems, in-

Even with modern tools, present-day totem pole building still requires a great deal of skill and precision.

corporating a box at the top of the figure to hold the remains.

Only woodcarvers who were recognized as master craftsmen were commissioned by chiefs to make a totem pole. Although others joined the carver in thanking the selected tree for giving itself as a totem pole, helped cut down the tree by means of fire, ax, and adze, and helped carry it to a designated spot, the carver alone designed and carved the totems. Necessity demanded he participate in the summer gathering season, so carving work was done primarily in the winter.

Let the Celebration Begin: Potlatches

Winter was not only a time of remembering those who had passed on, but also a time of thanks for bounty and for celebrating important life-changing events. The Indians combined these times with a huge party called a potlatch. The word comes from *patshatl* which means "gift giving" in the jargon used by inland Northwest tribes that traded with the totem pole people. But a potlatch was more than merely a party where the host gave gifts to his guests.

Interpreting a Totem Pole

Several animals carved on totem poles may be easily identified, such as frogs. But it can be harder to tell whether a bird is a raven or a thunderbird. Carvers did not always keep animal body parts in an anatomically correct location—sticking extra eyes or feet and claws here or there—so experts are still debating the identity of some animals on ancient poles. A few clues help. A raven has a slightly bent beak. A beaver has large upper teeth and a crisscrossed tail. A killer whale has a dorsal fin. Although there are different interpretations of which animal is which when it gets to similar animals such as otters and seals, historians agree that the art form of totem poles is fascinating.

Interpreting what a totem pole represents can often be a difficult task.

Historian Norman Bancroft-Hunt, who offers a succinct definition of this unique institution of the totem pole Indians, says that the potlatch "was used to validate social rank by a claimant to a position of privilege demonstrating that he had sufficient wealth to maintain the position."[16] Many times a potlatch justified a new chief's inheritance. The testimonial of the chief's right to a name and power in front of witnesses served a judicial-political function as an oral record in a society that had no written word. This process could be compared to the modern-day practice of notarizing a document or registering a deed. The gift giving was to thank the guests for witnessing the transfer of power.

Because giving gifts was an important part of a potlatch, the event was planned for months, with members of a chief's household and family contributing bounty to the accumulated potlatch goods. Sometimes the amassing of enough gifts to give away took more than a year. Even if the party was a memorial potlatch to mourn a dead chief and celebrate the new chief, the event could not be rushed. The new chief assumed responsibilities and status soon after the death of his predecessor but awaited the proper time to show others publicly that he was the chosen leader.

Many times other life-changing events were announced at a memorial potlatch, which might last several days. The birth of a child, the puberty and coming-out notice of a girl of noble status, and a marriage all required ceremony at a potlatch. These ac-

Potlatches were held to validate social rank and to celebrate marriages, births, and other important, life-changing events.

tivities occasionally merited a potlatch of their own. Potlatches had their own protocol and etiquette, and they differed in style from the northern nations to the southern nations, but their intent was the same.

A Kwakiutl Indian explains this tradition: "When one's heart is glad, he gives away gifts. It was given to us by our Creator, to be our way of doing things, we who are Indians. The potlatch was given to us to be our way of expressing joy."[17]

The Guests Arrive on Time— And Not Before

Typically, chiefs from neighboring villages and other tribes were invited to a potlatch by envoys of the host chief. A chief and his party who had to travel a hundred miles or more were likely to arrive before the appointed day. When this happened, the early guests camped a mile or so down the beach from the host village. On the first day of the potlatch, they loaded up the canoes and paddled back into the ocean to await the arrival of guests from the immediate vicinity. Then all the guests headed for the village to be formally welcomed by official greeters and wooden figures marking the host's beach.

The first day of the potlatch was filled with renewing old friendships among the hundred or more guests, feasting, watching

Dancing, songs, and other performances were only a small part of a potlatch.

dramatic performances, more feasting, playing games of chance, and still more feasting. High-ranking guests slept in the host chief's home; others slept outside in temporary lean-to shelters.

Raising the Totem Pole

Many potlatches included raising a totem pole as part of the ceremony. On the day of the raising, the chief or his speaker held a speaker's staff, an ornately carved stick featuring the chief's totems, and tapped it to request silence. When the people had quieted down, they were seated according to rank to listen as the raising of the pole was announced. While the guests chanted along with the rhythmic beat of drums and rattles, the pole-raising crew dragged the log, with the figures facing the sky, to the prepared trench-and-hole. The pole was raised by a leverage-and-tackle method, and all exclaimed in admiration.

Again the chief tapped his speaker's staff for quiet. Then he explained each crest, figure, and totem on the pole, which recounted the history of his lineage, and gave the several reasons for the potlatch.

The Ceremony of Privilege

The party would move inside the chief's house, where again the guests were seated according to their rank. Stories of the chief's heritage were told. Dances and songs that belonged to his family were performed. Individuals of lesser rank than the chief, including commoners, were given names or privileges. In some cases, the ears of boys and girls were pierced. Girls' lips were cut to receive their first labret, a lip ornament. Talents were recognized. A boy might be apprenticed to a master totem pole carver. A child who had displayed spirit power might be given to a shaman for tutelage.

Always there was feasting. It was essential that there be an excess of food. It showed that the host chief had wealth that could be disposed of without a care. Eating contests were held, sometimes with a canoe full of food as the bounty to be eaten.

A fire in the center of the large house was fed by fish oil so that the flames licked the ceiling. Guests seated close to the fire did not shy away from the heat. To do so would be to admit they were hot, which would show a weakness. The Indians sought envy and admiration and would save face at whatever the cost, even a few singed hairs.

When it was time to give away gifts, the chief or his speaker began by presenting the more valued items, such as a Chilkat robe or a canoe, to the highest ranking guest. On occasion a copper, a hammered sheet of rare copper nuggets and the most important item a chief could own, was given away or destroyed to show that wealth meant nothing to the potlatch host. Tallymen kept track of each item and to whom it was given. Sea otter pelts, furs, blankets, dried fish, baskets, boxes, and ornaments were among the gifts. Everyone, even the lowest ranking guest, received something.

The end of the gift giving signaled the end of the potlatch. Satiated guests would load their canoes with their presents and push off for their homes. They knew at their own future potlatch they would be expected to give to their host gifts as good as they had received. That was the way of the social prestige system. That was their way of life.

Chapter 4

Religion, Ceremonies, and Spirits

For the Indians blessed with an environment that provided their needs of food and shelter, there was leisure time to wonder, as countless other societies have done, how the world came to exist. Throughout the Pacific Northwest Coast, Native Americans believed in a Supreme Being, but the idea of one God was rather vague. The character and personality of the Supreme Being were unknown, and although it was the habit of most coastal Indians to deliver a morning prayer to a deity associated with the sky, there were no group worship services at specified times and places.

All the people believed, however, that everything in nature possessed a spirit. A stone on the shore, a tree, a fish, the sun, the moon, stars, lakes, rivers, animals, and each person—all had a power source within. Native Americans believed that spirits of living creatures did not forever cease to exist when the body died. Rather, they believed in life renewal: just as new growth sprang from the trunk of a felled tree, other spirits might come back again and again.

The Return of the Dead

Most of the people along the coast feared that the dead would return as ghosts to seize the unlucky and take them to the Land of the Dead. This was a place far away, where ghosts enjoyed a lifestyle similar to the one they had left, but on a different plane.

Life after death was believed to flow along multiple pathways. The Tlingit believed the ghost of a person settled around the cremated remains. Another spirit of the deceased went forever to the Land of the Dead. Yet another spirit of the same individual was reincarnated in a baby born before the deceased's memorial potlatch. The Kwakiutl placed their dead in boxes and tied them high in trees or placed them in caves. They believed that people went to a lower world for four years (by which time their bodies would have largely decayed), whereupon they would be reincarnated.

The spirit world remained close to all the coast Indians, and when death occurred inside a house, it was customary to remove the body through an opening created by taking boards from the side of the building. By preventing the ghost from exiting through the front door, the Indians kept the living from traveling on the path of the dead as they entered and exited the house. This would insure that the ghost did not return on his path to take the living back with him to the Land of the Dead for companionship.

The Supernatural

Because they were relatively unfamiliar with the forests and mountains, the Indi-

ans believed that supernatural creatures dwelled in these regions. Here lived the monsters, dwarfs, giants, and other fantastic supernatural characters who supposedly preyed on humans. These creatures could also change shape, taking on the guise of humans and benevolent-looking animals to entice people to their lairs, where the people would meet an awful death.

The sea and river also contained supernatural monsters, but the Indians felt more at home in these areas and were not as fearful of the marine creatures. In fact, seeing a two-headed sea monster was believed by some to be a sign of good luck.

The Indians of the Northwest Coast believed that everything in nature possessed a spirit that continued to exist even after the body died.

Controlling Spirits Through Rituals

Secular and religious life were inseparable to the Indians. Power might be part of the spirit world, but it was apparent in nature everywhere one looked. For example, heavy rains had to have a cause, so people told stories of Thunderbird, a giant bird that created thunder when it moved its wings. A tree struck by lightning or an unusual rock formation was believed to mean that something supernatural had occurred on the site. Similarly, whistling wind in the trees or the roar of underground water meant a spirit was close at hand. The Indians believed the unseen forces around them could be influenced by conduct and

ritual. That is, they expected that if they treated spirits in a just way, the spirits would return. Thus they observed the first salmon rites to show respect to the salmon, and they thanked a whale for bringing all its valuable food and oil to shore. In a comparable manner, they showed respect and gratitude to other animals they trapped or hunted.

The Indians thanked a bear for giving its life so that they might have fresh meat and warm fur. In many areas, when a bear's body was brought into the house, it would be welcomed with speeches. Sometimes the carcass was seated in a place of honor for a day or two, like a guest. The Nootka tied a bear in an upright position behind the house and lay salmon at its feet. Then a chief sprinkled the bear with eagle down and said, "We have waited for you to visit us for a long time. Here is the eagle down you came to get."[18]

The Bella Coola used another approach: they skinned the bear, placed the fur backward on the carcass, patted it four times and said, "Tell your brothers, your sisters, your uncles, your aunts, and your other relatives to come to me."[19] This treatment was intended to guarantee that the bear's spirit would return in a kind fashion and not in a threatening way. Returning the bones to the place where the

A tree struck by lightning was believed to mean that something supernatural had occurred on the site.

Benefits of a Guardian Spirit

Over a hundred known guardian spirits provided Native Americans of the Pacific Northwest with many attributes. Each spirit was known for a specific quality. The following are a few examples:

Guardian spirits such as the bear (pictured) provided men and women with various attributes.

Bear provided women with industriousness and skill at housekeeping and motherhood. He gave men the gift of great endurance as skilled hunters.

Beaver gave medicine power. By chanting his song, a recipient could change snow or cold weather to rain or mist.

Mountain Goat made the Indian fleet-footed and a good climber.

Owl gave his strength to fishing, primarily for sturgeon, but also halibut and salmon.

Seal provided the Indian with swimming ability and fishing skill.

animal had died was also believed to prevent the spirit from returning with animosity toward the hunter.

The Indians believed everything—from war, hunting and fishing, basket weaving, and canoe building—could be aided by the supernatural if the proper forms were observed. Sometimes a simple prayer was enough. Other times specific rituals had to be observed. Going to a sacred spot or using a special charm might be all that was required. To gain courage for war, a chief

might bathe in salt water where he believed supernatural sharks lived.

Not upsetting the spirits required ritual cleanliness; human body odors were considered offensive to spirits. Most Indians bathed regularly so that if they accidentally ran into a spirit, they would be prepared.

Spirit Quests

To earn the protection of a spirit or to obtain special powers, such as hunting or fishing skills, a person had to seek out a spirit and then challenge and dominate it until the desired power had been granted. If the spirit was not dominated, it might possess the seeker instead, which could lead to insanity or death.

A spirit quest was normally made by children before the onset of puberty. They were trained for these solitary vigils. From the ages of five or six, they took daily baths, even in the coldest of weather. Adults taught them to overcome fear of the woods, where many spirits were believed to dwell, by asking them to retrieve items from certain points. A special object

might be placed on the top of a hill or beside a lake. The child would go out at night, locate the object, and return it.

From the age of around ten, boys and girls would begin the first of their spirit quests. They had been taught which of the hundred-plus spirits favored their family, and normally these were the ones they sought. Not every quest was successful, and children seldom knew if they had received a special power until after they reached adulthood, usually in their thirties.

Before a spirit quest, a child had to take extreme caution and follow a prescribed ritual. First, he or she had to en-

A young Haida boy prepares to embark on a spirit quest. From the age of around ten, boys and girls would begin spirit quests.

dure a fast, followed by a total cleansing performed according to the step-by-step rite that belonged to the family. The child bathed in cold water for several hours in a special location for a specified number of days, usually four, and during particular phases of the moon. The bath was followed by a vigorous body rub with sweetly scented branches or plants that removed any traces of the offensive human odor. This rubbing restored circulation, but many times the process was so violent that it caused the skin to bleed.

Now in a state of semiconsciousness brought on by lack of food, exposure to cold, and loss of blood, the child would offer prayers and eagle down to the spirit. This might go on for days before an unusual noise attracted the attention of the seeker, who might see an animal that looked a little different than normal. This abnormal look would signify that this was indeed a spirit that had taken an animal form. If the seeker could hit the animal with a stick, known as killing the spirit, then the spirit would leave a token of its power. Many times the Indian on the quest fainted at this point.

Children were given advice on how to deal with this terrifying experience. In *Keepers of the Totem,* an Indian woman recalls the instructions given to her:

> You may hear a voice, but don't run away. Stay and listen. Then when you start home, don't run, just walk slowly. If you pass a pool or a stream, stop and swim. Dive five times. Then if you are tired, lie down, but be sure you are on the side

Nootkan Wolf Dance

The Nootkan's secret society involved the entire village and was a serious celebration of an old legend interspersed with humorous horseplay, feasting, and frivolity. Children were kidnapped by the wolf people (members dressed in wolf pelts and masks) and taken to a place to be taught special dances. At the end of four days, during which the villagers feasted and danced, the wolf people would appear on great rafts with their charges. The villagers would attack, and the wolf people would counterattack. These attacks would alternate back and forth until the children were rescued. Each child then performed the special dance and song he or she had been taught and revealed the special name he or she had been given.

of the water toward home. If you hear a voice again, don't be frightened. Stay and listen. The spirit will not cross the water; it will stay on the other side. It will be an animal when you first see it, but it will change and look like a man. It will tell you what power you will have and what you are to do when you are grown.[20]

The child might not remember much of what occurred on the spirit quest. Subsequent dreams later in life would reveal the full power that the spirit had given to the

Indian. Also during dreams, the spirit would teach the Indian its special dances, songs, and face painting. Once aware of what his gift was, an Indian might practice for months or years before mastering the ability granted to him. These special powers varied from the ability to make a whale drift ashore to the ability to split wood straight and true. This guardian spirit might also protect the seeker from evil spirits.

Becoming a Shaman

Males and females who had attained the most power from intense vision quests underwent a long training period and became shamans. These medicine men and women served as intermediaries between the supernatural realm and the Indians. A shaman was respected because of his or her extraordinary talent in curing illness, a shaman's primary function. Many a shaman could also control the weather, guarantee success for warriors, and predict the future.

Parents looked for signs that their child might be shaman material. If a child stayed off to him- or herself instead of playing with others, went into trances or had fits, or was visited by a mouse (the Indians believed a mouse could speak all languages), he or she might grow up to be a shaman. Many times this incredible link to the supernatural ran in families.

An account of the apprenticeship of a mid-nineteenth-century Coast Salish shaman appears in *Keepers of the Totem*. When the shaman was only three, his mother, a medicine woman, made him bathe in icy water and scrub himself with spruce limbs. Then she announced that she was clothing him with her power, to give him strength and special powers. Until he was ten, he lived like other children, playing and learning life skills. Then it was time to train for the chosen profession. He was sent to the woods for daylong periods to bathe, walk, and pray. Other shamans instructed him in their ways. Soon he was staying overnight in the woods, and his ventures lengthened. He spent much of the next four years alone. Then a vision came to him:

> I had been dancing and had fallen to the ground exhausted. As I lay there, sleeping, I heard a medicine man singing far, far away, and my mind traveled toward the voice. Evil medicine men seemed to swarm around me, but always there was someone behind me who whispered, "Pay no attention to them, for they are evil." And I prayed constantly to Him Who Dwells Above, asking for power to heal the sick, not to cause sickness as did these evil ones.[21]

A shaman was not a part of the ranked social system, but was outside it. Still, there were levels of prestige within the shaman society based on the identity of a shaman's spirit helpers. A shaman was feared as well as respected because tribe members assumed he or she had the power to harm them as well as help them. A shaman did nothing to dissuade this belief.

In the north, shamans were easily recognized because of their wild hairdos. Instead of combing their hair, they mixed in paint and bird down, with a tangled mess as the result. In the southern regions, shamans had a more conventional appearance, but everyone knew of their identities and of their special cures.

Shamanic Diagnosis: A Cautious Procedure

Although a shaman's principal duty was to heal the sick, diagnosis and treatment

A shaman examines a sick man prior to pronouncing his diagnosis.

were viewed as two separate functions. Usually a shaman was called to a sick person's house by relatives after herbs and healing remedies had failed and the patient was very ill. The shaman then examined the patient through a series of pokes and prods before giving his or her opinion. Historian Philip Drucker paraphrases a typical diagnosis:

> It's a pity, but I'm afraid your kinsman is too far gone; he will probably die no matter what I do. I could have cured him without a doubt if you had called me in time, but now his ailment has progressed too far. Of course, if you wish, I'll do what I can, but I can't promise to save him.[22]

Such a speech almost invariably resulted in relatives begging the shaman to try a cure, which he or she then did, having protected him- or herself no matter what the outcome. If the patient died, the shaman had been called too late; if the patient lived, the shaman was quite the hero and had cured a person on the brink of death.

Some shamans gave a more detailed diagnosis, preceded by singing over the patient, shaking special rattles, and dancing. Northern shamans wore exquisitely carved wooden masks representing familiar spirits. When a shaman could finally "see" what ailed the patient, as if looking though a transparent body, the shaman could pause and decline to take the case if he or she considered it too difficult. The shaman could claim that the patient was too near death or beyond his or her specialty, in which case he or she might recommend another shaman.

A Shaman's Day at the Office

As the shaman began the cure, relatives, friends, and neighbors gathered to watch the ritual. For example, if the diagnosis pinpointed an illness caused by a foreign object inside the body, the shaman danced to a drum, chanted, and seemed to extract objects by sucking with his or her mouth

or a tube, or by massaging the area and pretending to reach inside. Each shaman had a particular routine, and each one had personal sleight-of-hand tricks used to produce an illness-causing object. Sometimes there really was a fish bone, button, or other foreign object to be extracted and shown to family and friends. Usually, though, there was no such article, and so the shaman claimed that the cause of the illness was visible only to him- or herself. In such cases, the shaman showed the family a ball of eagle down soaked in blood. Unbeknownst to the observers, the shaman had been concealing this substitute all along. Not showing the actual object was not considered dishonest. After all, the

After diagnosing an illness, a shaman would attempt to extract foreign objects from a body by sucking them out through a sucking tube.

shaman had been given the power by the spirits to make the object visible to others by means of any special effects he or she might choose.

A more serious diagnosis was "soul loss." Only specialists, certain powerful shamans, could recover a lost soul for a patient who was lethargic and wasting away. Usually the shaman worked alone, but to effect the most dramatic of recoveries, shamans around the Puget Sound area would call in other shamans to take him or her to the Land of the Dead to find the soul.

With these assistant shamans holding painted boards representing a supernatural canoe, the specialist shaman made a symbolic voyage to the Land of the Dead, searched until the soul was located, and then restored it to the patient. A shaman's expressions and jerking motions while going into a trancelike state were interpreted by the witnesses as physical manifestations of what the shaman was seeing. If the shaman's hands were waving fitfully, he or she was fighting to escape the Land of the Dead. Whether this elaborate cure or a simple foreign object removal was performed, it was necessary to pay the shaman.

Some Indians felt that the more payment a shaman was given, the harder he or she would work. In more recent times, a shaman retorted to that charge, "This is the way of the true medicine man. When he is treating a patient, he pays no attention to the amount of money or blankets that the people offer him; if his patient dies, he returns everything that has been given to him."[23]

Still, shamans made a living from the business of healing. That shamans could sometimes be hired to work evil magic made Indians view them with suspicion, and when they died they were buried along with their box of rattles and soul catchers some distance from the village. Throughout their lifetime, however, shamans were treated with respect, for the Indians revered the spirits that occupied a central position in their culture.

The Supernatural Season

During the winter months, when little hunting or fishing could be done, even more time was devoted to nurturing relations with the spirit world. Indeed, the cold months were known as the "supernatural season," for it was then that the spirits were believed to be closest to the people, and Indians celebrated this connection with songs and dances. The ceremonies ranged from individual singing and dancing in the south to much more dramatic rites in the north.

In the southern areas, the Coast Salish were known for their Spirit Singing. At these huge get-togethers, as many as a hundred people might sing the personal Guardian Spirit songs, acquired during their spirit quests. Usually these were sung one at a time with drummers beating a rhythm as the dancer circled the longhouse. Men's dancing was frenzied and involved leaping. Women's dances were slower and more sedate. Dancers of both sexes were believed to be possessed by their spirits while they danced. Wolfgang Jilek, author of *Salish Indian Mental*

Present-day Tlingit participate in Spirit Singing. It is felt that Spirit Singing helps maintain close ties with nature.

Health and Culture Change, interviewed a dancer who described his participation in a Spirit Singing. Norman Bancroft-Hunt quotes a portion of this account:

> When you sing your breath starts shaking. After a while it goes into you. You try to sing, your jaws start to shake, then you sing it out, you get over it. When I dance, I don't act, just follow your power, just follow the way of your power.[24]

Spirit Singing was only one manifestation of the Indians' persistence in maintaining close ties with nature. Secret societies, which originated in the north, offered another means of accessing the spirit world.

Secret Societies

The Kwakiutl of the north were known for their secret dancing societies, and Indians of other nearby language groups adopted bits and pieces of the societies' rituals. The Kwakiutl had three distinct societies: the Shamans, Those-Who-Descend-from-the-Heavens, and the Dog-Eaters. Different spirits controlled the different societies. Membership was limited, and new people were accepted only when members died or retired from active participation.

For example, the dominant spirit of the Shamans' Society, whose membership included nonshamans, was Hamatsa, a cannibal. His ceremony, performed when the society needed to induct a new member, was an elaborately staged affair. The person designated as the initiate was kidnapped by other members and taken to a secret place to be instructed in the ways of the society. Parts of the initiation cere-

Tricks of the Dancing Societies

Informants have told anthropologists about the sleight-of-hand tricks and props that produced magical effects in the public dancing society ceremonies. Part of the initiation into a secret society involved the novice being caught by other tribe members before the actual indoor ceremonial dancing began. This was as prearranged as the actual ceremony. Many times a novice would appear at one end of the village, yelling like a cannibal. After the Indians took off in pursuit, he might appear at the other end of the village. A substitute, often a relative or slave, would have been the original decoy. A dramatic reappearance involved walking toward the village on the ocean side. The initiate would appear to be walking on water, but in reality he was walking on a raft, weighted down to below the surface of the water with heavy stones.

The ceremonial house had trapdoors and a secret room. Hollow kelp stems used as speaking tubes were buried under the floor with the ends at various places to throw ghostly voices.

mony were secret, and parts were public. During the public ceremony, members of the society wore carved wooden masks that disguised their identity.

Before the public ceremony, a wild-acting, spirit-possessed novice returned to the village, and after several attempts, was captured and taken into the specially prepared house for the ceremony. On his way inside, he bit an Indian or two to convince spectators that he was indeed possessed by a cannibal spirit.

Subdued by being tied to a pole, the initiate participated in a public winter dancing ceremony to exorcise the cannibal spirit from its human host. The ensuing frenzy came to a climax with the bringing out of a corpse for the initiate to eat. Although the cannibal feast appeared real, most historians agree that the society members faked this part of the ceremony by substituting a bear skin with a carved human face that passed as a human corpse in the dim firelight. Following this rite, the cannibal spirit was appeased, the novice regained his normal composure, and a potlatch was held to celebrate his initiation into the society. The initiate then underwent a purification time that could last as long as four years.

The traditional dancing ceremony of the Shamans' Society was held at most once a year. It joined the past to the present and encouraged solidarity of beliefs by those engaged in the dancing and those who observed. The winter ceremonies linked spirits and humans.

Chapter 5

The White Man Arrives

When the first white explorers in a huge ship sailed in sight of the Pacific Northwest Coast, legend says that the Indians believed it was a supernatural being, probably Raven. Historians disagree if the first tall ship to reach the area was sailed by Englishman Francis Drake in 1579 or by the Spaniards Lorenzo Ferrer Maldonado in 1588, Juan de Fuca in 1595, or Bartholemew de Fonte, who may have sailed up the coast from Mexico in 1640. None of these Europeans had an impact on the totem pole Indians. Rather, the first foreign influence was due to the ambitions of a Russian emperor.

The Fur Trade Begins

In 1741, a century after the voyage of de Fonte, Dane Vitus Bering, who had been commissioned by Peter the Great of Russia to search for a land connection between Asia and North America, set sail from Siberia with Russian Aleksey Chirikov. The two ships were separated by wind and fog. Chirikov sailed to Tlingit

territory, anchored, and sent two small boats of sailors to shore. Neither returned. Wanting to risk no more lives, he returned to Russia. Bering's crew found signs of a settlement on Kayak Island, but no Indians. Bering died before the ship set sail for home.

When Bering's ship returned to Russia bearing sea otter furs, a chain of events was set off that led to dire consequences for the Indians.

For years Russia had traded furs to China, exhausting the accessible wildlife supply in their vast land. Bering's evidence of sea otter off Kayak Island opened a new avenue, and trappers were quickly sent to the land north of the area claimed by the totem pole Indians. Years later Empress Catherine II of Russia informed European diplomats about the fur trade. In 1774 Spain sent Juan José Pérez from Mexico as far north as the Queen Charlotte Islands owned by the Haida. Pérez did not land, but traded with the Haida, who paddled their canoes out to see the strange vessel. His orders were to subdue the Indians so that they "may be bathed in the light of the Gospel by means of spiritual conquest."[25] But he did not communicate well with the Haida, nor trust them, and left after two days without putting into shore. His experience with the Nootka of Vancouver Island was similar.

The English Arrive

Four years later, in 1778, the English ships *Resolution* and *Discovery* under the command of Captain James Cook reached the Northwest. Journals kept during this journey provide historians with firsthand accounts of Cook's meetings with the Nootka. Second Lieutenant James King wrote that their ships were met by Nootka canoes.

[The crews] perform'd what seemed a necessary ceremony, which was pulling & making a circuit round both Ships with great swiftness, & their Paddles kept in exact time; one man would stand up in the middle with a Spear or rattle in his hand, & a mask on which was sometimes the figure of a human face, at others that of an Animal, & kept repeating something in a loud tone. At other times they would all join in a Song, that was frequently very Agreeable to the Ear, after this they always came alongside & began to trade without Ceremony.[26]

In answer to this type of welcome, Cook had his sailors play their fife, drum, and French horns. The Nootka, who valued

Bering's crew returned to Russia with sea otter furs. This act led to dire consequences for the inhabitants of the area.

selves with bear grease to prevent burns from the wind and sun, and they put grease in their hair to make small feathers stick to it for decoration. Face and body painting completed the look that so disconcerted the British explorers. Cook thought that in a more superstitious time, visitors to this land would see the Indians as "a race of beings partaking of the nature of man and beast."[28]

Cook went ashore and was amazed by the remarkable houses where many families lived in compartments divided by mats and boards. Other European explorers and traders also described the longhouses, although some may have tended toward exaggeration. English captain John Meares claimed he saw one house with great carved posts where eight hundred people lived. Another explorer, Simon Fraser, measured a Salish house and recorded it as fifteen hundred feet long and ninety feet wide. Explorer Alexander Mackenzie commented that the boards of the Bella Coola were so cleanly joined that they appeared to be made of one piece. He was impressed with the art of the Bella Coola houses, which he said "were painted with hieroglyphs and figures of different animals and with a degree of correctness which was not to be expected of such an uncultivated people."[29]

Mackenzie looked beyond the houses at the art and added, "But the sculpture of

Judging the culture as inferior, Captain James Cook was nevertheless impressed by the longhouses built by the Northwest Coast Indians.

songs and their traditions, responded favorably. King wrote, "These were the only people we had seen that ever paid the smallest attention to those or any of our musical Instruments."[27]

Captain Cook, like other Europeans of his time, believed that illiterate people had an inferior culture, and he did not understand the ways of the Indians. His impression of the natives was of dirty people wearing wooden masks. Because the Indians bathed so frequently, they were hardly dirty, but many times they covered them-

these people is superior to their painting." He further commented on the society of the Indians. "Of the many tribes of savage people I have seen, these appear to be the most susceptible of civilization."[30]

What the Indians Wanted

The Indians, for their part, were amazed by the bearded men in their "swimming houses," with their "magic sticks," or guns. But they were not so in awe that they did not recognize a good trading opportunity. They had traded among themselves for years. Now the white men wanted furs, and they traded as many as they could trap. Captain Cook wrote in his journal, "For these things they took in exchange, Knives, chissels, pieces of iron and Tin, Nails, Buttons, or any kind of metal. Beads they were not fond of and cloth of all kinds they rejected."[31]

Between 1785 and 1815 over 140 ships, mostly English and American, traded with the coastal people. Trade items had meaning for the Indians, but did not greatly change their way of life. Their acquisition of metal made their tools more useful and may have increased production of totem poles, boxes, and canoes, but it did not change the style. Once the demand for iron was met, the Indians began bartering for other items, and what they accepted once was not necessarily accepted the next time. New items did not replace old items, but merely supplemented them, even though it seemed that fad and fancy dictated the Indians' trade choices. For a while they accepted full-dress uniforms, which they used in their ceremonies in addition to their usual ornate cedar-bark and fur robes.

Although sailors realized that guns and ammunition might be used sooner or later against them or their countrymen, they traded those items for furs, and Indian villages soon amassed arsenals. It took some time for the Indians to become good shots, but the loud noise added to the confusion when a war party attacked a village. Raids were no longer merely to gain slaves or settle a dispute. Now the Indians fought over who would trade with the Europeans, and they pillaged to capture more pelts to trade.

Chinook Jargon

The Chinook, living just south of the Coast Salish, were master traders. They traded with interior tribes via their navigation on the Columbia River, which divides the present-day states of Washington and Oregon, and took interior goods to the coastal tribes. The Chinook took words and phrases from all the tribes they dealt with and combined them into a trading language which European traders also learned. For example: *Boston* stood for *Anglo-American; melass* for *molasses; tum-tum* for *heart;* and *potlatch* for *gift giving.* The vocabulary included over one thousand words.

Just as they had seen the advantages of firearms, the Indians admired the huge billowing sails of the tall ships and wondered at the ability to tame the wind. Indian canoes were superbly built and styled, but paddling was the only means of movement. Thus, until the market was glutted, the Indians traded for sails to attach to their canoes. Soon canoes were made with a projection on the floor for holding a mast and sails. Lacking a deep keel, a sail-equipped canoe could only run with the wind. But even without the ability to set sails to chart a course, life had become easier for the Indian paddlers.

Not all European customs found favor with the Indians, however. They disliked the Europeans' food, with a few exceptions. Sugar and molasses were quite popular, for the Indians' sweet tooth previously had been satisfied only by berries. In addition, Europeans introduced Native Americans to rum from the West Indies. Although the traders stretched the rum by watering it down, it was a novel intoxicant for the Indians.

Among the many changes to Native American society brought about by European explorers and those who came later, the presence of trading forts was to exert a particularly powerful impact.

Admiring the tall sails of the European ships, the Indians traded various items in order to obtain sails for their canoes.

Tlingit Helmets

Unlike the other Pacific Northwest Coast Indians, the Tlingit fiercely fought Europeans when they first settled in the area. Tlingits raided and burned two Russian forts. While fighting, Tlingit warriors covered their heads with carved wooden helmets. Likenesses of animals known for their fierceness and supernatural beings were carved on these helmets and then painted. The wooden creatures were to scare those being attacked and give supernatural powers to the Tlingit wearing the helmets.

Trading Forts Dot the Landscape

In the early 1800s, as sea otter were hunted nearly into extinction, trade shifted to other furs, including many land animals. Trading venues therefore shifted from small camps near ships to permanent forts. The Russian and British companies established such fortified settlements and claimed the surrounding land for their countries. For a brief time Spanish and American companies also ventured into trading outposts and land claims.

Russian fur traders continued to operate in the north and established forts in Tlingit territory without consulting Tlingit chiefs. This led to battles with Tlingit warriors, who captured and burned two settlements before the superior guns of the Russians subdued them.

The English North West Company prospered briefly with several small forts, but it was soon taken over by the powerful English Hudson's Bay Company, which built a line of forts from Tlingit territory in the north to areas south of those inhabited by totem pole Indians.

The switch from ships to forts caused the Indians to be treated differently. During ship trading times, a semihostile atmosphere prevailed. Indians took over some ships and would have taken over more if they had been as skilled and well armed as the Europeans. White traders quickly learned to permit only a few Indians aboard at a time, and occasionally they held a noble child hostage until trading was concluded. While anchored, a captain and crew might treat the Indians with respect and bargain with them for the furs. Yet as quotas were reached and time to set sail neared, some captains forcibly took furs they had not paid for. The Indians would take revenge for these thefts on the next unfortunate ship to arrive.

Once permanent forts were established, however, the traders had to bond with the Indians and forge a relationship that would last. It was necessary, for example, to cease relying on novelties or fad items as goods to be traded. The Hudson's Bay Company, with its vast experience with other Native Americans across the continent, was wise enough to supply blankets, which were readily accepted by the Indians as something

The establishment of trading posts led to an increased circulation of European goods among the Northwest Coast tribes.

approaching a monetary standard. The stability of a basic trade item helped achieve an economic base for the traders and Indians alike.

Deadly Diseases

Along with a new economic standard, Europeans introduced many diseases, starting with a smallpox epidemic as early as the 1770s when contact was first made. Every twenty or thirty years another deadly outbreak occurred among the young, who had acquired no immunities. An epidemic in the mid-1830s was devastating. Some historians estimate that smallpox and measles reduced the Indian population by half.

Others claim the number of deaths was much larger.

Further reducing the population was a form of illness previously unknown to the Indian people: venereal disease. In Indian society before Europeans came, chastity was cherished and prostitution virtually unknown. However, the Indians allowed their women to go to ships, lumber camps, and forts as prostitutes as long as their pay in blankets went toward the accumulation of wealth to use at a potlatch.

Rivalry Potlatches

With the deaths of so many Indians, positions of prestige were in constant flux.

When there was an inheritance dispute over a vacated chief's rank, the two rivals would feud with potlatches, each trying to out-give the other. The one who gave away more goods of high quality would assume the title.

The increase in wealth based on the new blanket economic system allowed potlatches to become an almost nightly affair. Where before a household took months and even years to amass the wealth necessary for a potlatch, now they were commonplace, and the competition was to give bigger and bigger potlatches. With the increased use of alcohol at the ceremonies, many times the traditional rituals were turned into drunken brawls. Such unruliness, combined with the hunger for land increasingly displayed by British and U.S. interests, led authorities on both sides of the Atlantic to step in and attempt to impose order.

Governments Begin Organizing the Area

With white settlers moving into lands previously claimed by Indians, white governments made treaties and policies without consulting the Indians. In 1846 the Treaty of Washington between Britain and the United States divided the Coast Salish lands in two at the forty-ninth parallel; the northern part was regarded as a British Royal Territory, and the southern part belonged to the United States.

By 1853 Washington Territory was created in the United States with Isaac I. Stevens appointed governor. He looked at the Coast Salish Indians as obstacles to the westward expansion of U.S. citizens, and he forced the Indians to sign treaties establishing reservations for them on a small portion of their lands and recognizing their ancestral fishing rights. He threatened the chiefs and told them if they refused to sign, soldiers would "wipe them off the earth."[32] Although the Indians were rebellious, their uprisings were soon put down, and they were forced to accept life on reservations—a fate that had befallen other Native American people in the wake of the Indian Relocation Act of 1830.

The British policy was less violent. Colonial governor James Douglas had been a fur trader and therefore knew a bit about Indian culture. He regarded Indians as "rational beings, capable of acting and thinking for themselves."[33] He believed the Indians had ownership rights and negotiated fourteen treaties for land on Vancouver Island. His plan for assimilating the Indians into landholders hinged on their accepting European religion and values.

Missionaries Move In

Traders had not tried to change the Indian way of life, but missionaries were determined to introduce Christianity. In the northern Tlingit areas, Russian Orthodox priests made some inroads. Priest Ivan Veniaminov in Sitka worked tirelessly to convert Indians and felt that priests should honor "ancient customs, so long as they are not contrary to Christianity."[34]

In the southern areas, Spanish Franciscan friars arrived in the 1830s and established Catholic missions. Because the Roman Catholic rituals appealed to the Indians' love of ceremonies, they were susceptible to this call of Christianity. Priests urged them to replace potlatches and shamanism with the pageantry of the Catholic liturgical cycle.

Protestant denominations also sent missionaries to convert the Indians. These religious people also shunned shamans and had a secret weapon to undermine mystic power: native medicine men could not cure smallpox, but the missionaries had vaccines against the disease. Despite making valuable contributions to public health, many of these missionaries thought totem poles were pagan idols that the Indians worshiped. Because of this misunderstand-

Beginning in the 1830s, Spanish Franciscan friars established Catholic missions among the Indians in the southern areas.

ing, many irreplaceable poles were cut down and burnt at the missionaries' insistence.

Enter William Duncan

No missionary had a bigger effect on the Indians than William Duncan, an Anglican layman who intended to convert and civilize the "barbarian, even cannibalistic savages."[35] He arrived in 1857 at Fort Simpson in Tsimshian territory. He was twenty-five years old. He concentrated on learning to communicate, not in the limited vocabulary of the Chinook Jargon used by the traders, but in the Tsimshian language.

He studied the Indians. He learned their myths and legends. Because one of their traditional narratives told of a great flood, Duncan built on this framework when he presented the biblical story of Noah. He came to understand the social structure, too, and he courted the chiefs. When he first began preaching the gospel, he knew that after he had spoken to prospective converts in one chief's house, other chiefs would ask him to appear in their houses to avoid losing prestige. He established a school to teach English, reading, writing, arithmetic, and religion. When some chiefs sent their children to school, commoners followed and sent their children to school, too.

Duncan made a few converts, but there were many Indians who taunted the new

Anglican missionary William Duncan was successful in establishing an Indian settlement apart from previous cultural influences. The settlement eventually came to resemble an English town.

Christians. How could Duncan expect his followers to abandon what he considered their heathen ways of potlatches and cannibal dances when they were surrounded by those who enjoyed those festivities? His answer was to take his chosen few away from the influence of their old culture.

A Christian Utopia

The site for this new venture was near Metlakatla Pass, an old winter village site of the Tsimshian. Some fifty converts made the trip after filling their canoes with tools, provisions, and European-style clothing. They left behind wooden masks, rattles, and other symbols of Tsimshian culture. Two days after they left Fort Simpson, a strong smallpox epidemic hit the fort. Shaman medicine was ineffective against this deadly disease, and many Tsimshian took this as a sign from above and joined Duncan's group. Several hundred Indians began building the new settlement in 1862.

Duncan welcomed all who were willing to abide by his rules, which included numerous prohibitions. For example, the people were not to indulge in

the Demoniacal Rites called Ahlied or Medicine Work; Conjuring and all the heathen practices over the sick;

Use of intoxicating liquor; Gambling; Painting Faces; Giving away property for display; Tearing up property in anger or to wipe away disgrace.[36]

Furthermore, they were to attend school and church, be clean and honest, give up clan obligations, and work for the good of the community.

Duncan established an outstanding town that resembled an English village. The Indians built a sawmill, a school, two-story houses with windows, a soap works, a brick kiln, and a salmon saltery, the forerunner of fish canneries. The cathedral was immense and purported to be the biggest west of Chicago.

Indians were required to contribute to the community in taxes as well as with good deeds. They served as policemen, firemen, and village councilmen, and played in the village brass band. Remembering the Indians' love of ceremony and competition, Duncan allowed special festivals with speeches and parades, which took the place of the potlatch and dancing societies. Duncan's town was such a success that he was consulted by both the British and American governments about Indian affairs.

Trouble in Paradise

Duncan's Metlakatla was such a model community that the Church Missionary Society, which had sent him to the Tsimshian in the first place, now saw fit to send a bishop. Duncan was dismayed, for although he publicly insisted that the Indians were partners in an elective-type government, he was the undisputed king. Unsurprisingly, he and the bishop were soon at loggerheads, and it was Duncan who had to leave. With the permission of the U.S. government, in 1887 he took several hundred Metlakatlan residents and established a New Metlakatla on Annette Island, a part of Alaska that had been sold by the Russians to the United States twenty years earlier.

The new town developed much like the old, this time with a fish cannery. But as he grew older, Duncan could not control his followers. After his death, tensions grew, for his charismatic personality had held the group together. Another church formed on the island, and this factionalism caused community-owned projects to fail.

Duncan had shown the totem pole Indians that they could be self-supporting. But some historians believe the breakup of the community based on this principle was a result of too much cultural change, acquired so rapidly that it could not take root.

Chapter 6

Changing Cultures

As more and more Europeans moved into the coastal region of the Pacific Northwest, Native Americans suffered a crisis of identity. Their summer gathering-and-storing way of life was being destroyed as their land was settled by strangers. Their culture

A Tlingit totem stands next to an abandoned military cannon in present-day Sitka, Alaska.

with its potlatches and mystical dances was dismissed by missionaries as pagan. And two separate governments were dictating laws under which they should live.

The United States Rules

In Washington Territory, reservations were established for tribes of the Coast Salish in the 1850s. Indians there were declared the wards of the government and were not considered U.S. citizens.

In 1867, the Russians sold Alaska to the United States for $7.2 million. The Tlingit, who had winter villages around Sitka, were aware of the sale. An intertribal meeting of chiefs objected, pointing out that the Russians did not own Indian land and therefore had no right to sell it. But with no force behind their objections, the Indians' voices were not heard.

Military Rule in Alaska

The first U.S. administration in Alaska was under the War Department. Jeff C. Davis, the army general in charge, was directed to impress upon the Indians and especially upon their chiefs, that our government will regard them as subject to its laws and entitled to its protection; that while they are protected by our government they will be required to respect the rights of all citizens of the republic; and that if any member of a tribe maltreat a citizen of the United States, the whole tribe and especially its chief, will be held responsible for the offense or crime committed by one of its members, unless they expel such criminal or deliver him to us for punishment.[37]

The army was largely ineffective in regulating Indian behavior. However, in 1869, the military made its might felt. Some Tlingit Indians from a Kuiu tribe killed two American prospectors, and the government exacted revenge. A navy warship anchored beside the Kuiu village. As the Indians had done since their first contact with traders, they ran into the woods, beyond the reach of the ship's guns. But once the village had been shot up, the sailors did not leave. Instead, they went ashore and smashed and burned canoes and houses. Before they were finished with their mission, they had destroyed eight villages. The Indians were not harmed, but their villages were devastated. They had nothing left—no houses and no tools to rebuild them with, no stores of fish and no canoes to catch more. Grieving and subdued, the Indians scattered to live with relatives in other tribes. The U.S. government had very effectively let the Indians know who was in charge.

The army command was withdrawn in 1877, and the navy took over. After all, the Indians lived in a coastal society, which was easier to control with a warship in sight. Navy commanders were much more hands-on in their dealings with the Indians. They learned the hierarchy of clan organization, and they applied pressure on the Indians to settle differences with payments instead of wars and long-running feuds. They also demanded that all Indian children attend mission schools, and they raided the stills in which Indians had been brewing *hoochino,* a foul-tasting but intoxicating drink made of fermented apples and berries mixed with water and flour.

Missionaries Influence the Indians

The Presbyterian Board of Home Missions first started a girls' school at Wrangell, Alaska, in 1877, but soon expanded to seven schools for both girls and boys and even a few adults, who voluntarily attended. Congressional aid for education in the Alaskan Territory supplemented the mission schools, and within a few years there was a school in every Indian village.

Missionaries, who were sponsored not only by the Presbyterians but also by the Society of Friends (Quakers), the Methodists, and the Salvation Army, saw education as the way of converting Native Americans to the Christian faith. Historian Philip Drucker aptly summed up the prevailing missionary attitude:

U.S. Navy officers pose with a gun aboard their warship. In 1869, the military made its might felt by completely destroying a Kuiu village.

[F]acility in English and the three R's, was *the* solution to [what the U.S. government referred to as] the Indian problem, a crucial phase of the program aimed at detribalizing the Indian and changing him into a sober, peaceful copy of a white man. Just where he would fit into white society was not clearly expressed.[38]

The churches also taught tenets of self-government by organizing clubs that needed elected officers, committees, and bylaws.

Acculturation intensified in Alaska with enterprises hiring Native Americans for jobs. A few fish canneries were established, and who better to work with fish than the people whose lives were built around the catching and preserving of fish? Native Americans were also hired as guides during the late 1800s gold rush years when miners swept through the area.

Who Gets the Land?

The first Organic Act for Alaska in 1884 provided civil law for the territory and extended federal mining laws. Prospectors staked off land which Native Americans had considered theirs. Indians were allowed only lands "in actual use and occupance,"[39] which usually meant home sites and gardens. Whites were allowed to file "squatter's claims" of 160 acres. Native Americans were not afforded squatter's rights.

Fish canneries jumped into the land-claim business. A cannery owner would

Fish canneries were built on the best salmon-spawning rivers, severely curtailing the Indians' freedom and eventually forcing them to work for wages in the canneries.

file for eighty acres on each side of a salmon stream, build his cannery, and deny fishing rights to anyone he wished to ban. By 1890, canneries had been built on every major salmon-spawning river. Native Americans might be allowed to fish on the streams after the cannery had its fill, but the owner also had the right to denounce them as trespassers. Now survival demanded that many Native Americans go to work for wages in the canneries, thus furthering their acculturation.

The Bureau of Education Steps In

By 1900, new legislation providing for territorial schools for white children was passed, and funds were appropriated for

Indian education as well. With the new administration came new policies, including the consolidation of schools.

The Haida of Prince of Wales Island had not banded together, and small villages dotted the shoreline. The Bureau of Education sought ways to cut costs and settled on moving the Haida into one area, which would mean only one large school instead of several small ones. By persuasion, the Bureau managed to relocate nearly all the Haida into the community of Hydaburg.

Children at Indian schools were punished if caught speaking their native Haida or Tlingit. This was one further way of eradicating the old ways and assimilating the Indians into white culture.

Alaska Native Brotherhood

The Indians were being molded into whites, but they did not have the rights of whites. They were not even citizens. To lobby for citizenship, nine Tlingits and one Tsimshian from New Metlakatla founded the Alaska Native Brotherhood in Sitka in 1912. All ten charter members were products of Presbyterian schools, and all ten worked toward the assimilation of the Indians into white culture. Three years later an organization for women, the Alaska Native Sisterhood, was established.

The Brotherhood showed that the Indians could work together for the common good, and they organized grassroots groups called "camps" in most villages. One issue that occupied them was racial discrimination. Not only were the separate schools for Indians second-rate, but local policies kept Indians out of stores and restaurants owned by whites. Signs were posted: "No Dogs or Natives Allowed."[40]

Through efforts of the Brotherhood, the Alaskan Indians were made U.S. citizens in 1922, two years before Indians in the continental states were granted the right to vote. The Brotherhood stepped up their demands for equality with whites, as well as becoming active in labor disputes and raising the issues of who owned their ancestral lands and why no payment was made for confiscated lands. By the late 1930s a movement was born to restore totem poles and copy those that were beyond repair, a sign that the Indians were looking back at what they had lost of their heritage and were determined to regain it.

Other organizations of Native Americans cropped up before and after Alaska became a state in 1958. These groups pressed demands for an answer to the land question, which prompted the Bureau of Indian Affairs to take a census of Tlingit and Haida. In addition, a federal committee was set up to study Native American land claims. The Alaskan Federation of Natives and Senator Fred Harris of Oklahoma drafted a national bill which negated the "actual use" of land policy of earlier Congresses. Senator Harris said, "We

Who Is an Indian?

The Indian Act of 1876 that applied to the Indians in British Columbia defined an Indian in strange ways. If an Indian woman married a white man, she was no longer considered a "status Indian." Nor were her children considered Indians. If she and an Indian husband had a child, and if the father died and she then married a white man, her full-blood child also would not be considered an Indian. If an Indian male married a white woman, she would be considered an Indian. This bizarre set of definitions reflected the concern of the Canadian government to prevent the reservations from being overrun by white men.

An amendment to the Indian Act in 1985 allowed Indian women to reclaim their status.

Women and children sit outside the Metlakatla Senior Citizens Center. The residents, who had reservation status, were excluded from the 1971 Alaska Native Claims Settlement Act.

know that the native people need vast areas of land if they are to continue their traditional way of life."[41] In 1968 the Tlingit-Haida Central Council won a lawsuit against the government resulting in payment of over $7.5 million plus 2.5 million acres of land as settlement.

Reaching More Settlements

In 1971, the Alaska Native Claims Settlement Act was passed, which extinguished aboriginal title to the land forever, including Indian claims as well as those of the Eskimos and Aleuts. Not included in this landmark settlement was the Tlingit-Haida Central Council, which had been compen-

sated in the 1968 settlement. Also excluded were the residents of New Metlakatla, who had reservation status. Forty million acres of land, $462.5 million (received over eleven years), plus an additional $500 million from mineral revenues were to be managed by twelve regional corporations controlled by the natives. The act also defined a native as a person with one-quarter native blood; if there was no proof, a person regarded as a native by a village that also regarded his or her parents as native was accepted as a native.

Over sixteen thousand Tlingit and Haida Indians are now stockholders in the successful Sealaska Corporation formed to administer their funds from the 1971 settlement. The corporation holds investments in forest products, financial markets, plastics, and mineral exploration and development, and pays a dividend to its shareholders. The corporation sees itself as a "strong, continuing link with our land, which has supported the Native culture for hundreds of generations."[42]

In Washington State, where reservations had earlier been established, there were still questions about state fishing restrictions, which were held to violate the treaties granting the Indians the right to fish at their "usual and accustomed grounds."[43] In 1974, a federal ruling upheld the treaties. Within ten years, one

The English government referred to the territory of British Columbia (pictured) as being "wild and unoccupied."

small Coast Salish tribe was responsible for one-fourth of all the fish caught in the state.

Although the totem pole Indians in Alaska have settled the land question and are U.S. citizens with full rights, many still struggle with prejudice and the acculturation process. They are working to find a balance between their heritage and the ways of white society. The history of Native American tribes in Canada has been somewhat different.

The Indians in British Columbia

On Canada's Vancouver Island during colonial days, treaties with the First Nations, as the Indians are called, had been negotiated. These stated that they could hunt and fish on their lands as they had before the colony had been established. The rest of the territory of British Columbia was referred to officially by the English government as "wild and unoccupied."[44] England failed to negotiate land treaties with the Indians in this colony, a departure from British practice in dealing with North American Indians elsewhere.

When British Columbia became a province in the dominion of Canada in 1871, Canadian federal laws went into effect. Still, there were no treaties with the First Nations in British Columbia, and it was now up to the

Dominion government to act. By establishing large reserves, the federal government in Ottawa hoped to settle the Indian question. But for this to occur, officials in the province would have to agree on the amount of land to be set aside for the Indians.

However, there was no agreement. The provincial government did not want large reserves established. It felt that the land in actual use was all the Indians needed. This land included their winter villages, summer fishing stations, and cemeteries. Policymakers in Ottawa, the Canadian capital, leaned toward allowing eighty to one hundred acres per family. Missionaries wanted the Indians to be given title to the same amount of land that was apportioned the white settlers. This would help the missionaries mold the Indians to fit into the white world and accept Christianity.

But what about the Indians? They knew their land boundaries, based on centuries-old traditions. The land was more than a place to settle; it was holy and it was theirs. They listened to the missionaries, the only ones who seemed to care about them or their problems.

With the encouragement of the missionaries, the Indians protested when the government surveyors measured their lands, but their objections were unavailing. When tracts were set aside as small reserves for the Indians, however, there was such sparse white settlement that the Indians were able to continue to roam their old lands as before. In any event, the land issue was replaced by another issue. The Indian Act of 1876 sweepingly declared all Indians across the continent as Canadian nationals, but they were regarded as wards, not as citizens. As wards of Canada, the Indians expected further interference with their traditional ways, and it was not long in coming.

The Potlatch Ban

Canadian Indian agents saw the feasting and giving away of property associated with potlatches as taking too much time, contributing to the Indians' idleness, and retarding acculturation. As Agent George Blenkinsop wrote, "These people are the richest in every respect in British Columbia and were a proper disposal made of their immense gains they could furnish themselves with every comfort they could possibly wish for."[45]

The Last Great Potlatch

In 1921, in defiance of the Canadian potlatch ban, Chief Daniel Cranmer of the Nimpkish tribe of Kwakiutl at Alert Bay held a huge six-day potlatch. At the end of the feasting, he distributed his wealth to some three hundred guests. The gifts included motorboats, pool tables, sewing machines, furniture, musical instruments, canoes, and cash. He was arrested, and many of those in attendance had to relinquish their goods, but he was proud that he had given the greatest potlatch ever.

The missionaries were also against the potlatch. They wanted it, as well as the secret dancing societies, stopped. In the missionaries' view, if Indians were to become Christian, they had to forsake their traditional culture. The Indians were told that their ways were wrong and those of white society were right. There was no in-between. This cultural arrogance left no room for attempts to understand the Indians' view of the purpose of acquired wealth, as expressed in the potlatch tradition.

In 1885, an amendment to the Indian Act banned the potlatch and the secret dancing societies. The Canadian government had forced underground an institution that was significant to the Indians' way of life. The potlatch speeches and dances were a means of teaching laws and history of the people. Some Indians defied the law and went to jail for short periods. Others distributed gifts under the cover of Christmas parties or went door-to-door handing out goods. Still others obeyed the law, letting their culture slip into disuse. The potlatch ban was not repealed until 1951. Meanwhile the land question resurfaced in Canada.

The Land Question Is Posed Again

In 1887, chiefs of the Nisga'a tribe of the Tsimshian traveled to Victoria, British Columbia, demanding a treaty and self-government. Chief David MacKay spoke to the investigating committee:

What we don't like about the Government is their saying this: "We will give you this much land." How can they give it when it is our own? We cannot understand it. They have never bought it from us or our forefathers. They say now that they will give us so much land—our own land. These chiefs do not talk foolishly, they know the land is their own, our forefathers' for generations. Chiefs have had their own hunting grounds, their salmon streams, and places where they got their berries; it has always been so. It is not only during the last four or five years that we have seen the land; we have always seen and owned it; it is no new thing, it has been ours for generations. If we had only seen it for twenty years and claimed it as our own, it would have been foolish, but it has been ours for thousands of years.[46]

The demand of the Nisga'a was dismissed, but it was the beginning of over a hundred years of petitions, discussions, and bargaining with the government for the rights to their land and control of their lives.

The Nisga'a took advantage of certain mechanisms of Anglo-Canadian jurisprudence in their attempts to further their land claims. In 1913, aiming to bypass the Canadian government, the Nisga'a sent a petition to the Privy Council in England, the highest court in the British Empire. The petition was not granted, but the ideas it embodied may have been the impetus behind the appointment that same year of a

Royal Commission to study the land question. After visiting every village, the commission recommended revisions, deletions or additions to Indian reserves, which were adopted by the provincial and dominion governments. The Nisga'a finally obtained a hearing before a Parliamentary committee in 1926, but the outcome was unsatisfactory. Their claim of aboriginal rights to the land was rejected.

The Land Question Remains Unresolved

For a while the land question was forgotten by the majority of coastal Indians in

Forced to assimilate into white society, some Indians became commercial fishermen.

Canada. They concentrated on adapting to life around them. Much as the Indians in Alaska, they worked at salmon canneries, and some became commercial fishermen, first using their own simple techniques, and later using more complex fishing methods and equipment. The logging industry also developed, affording jobs to Indians. Soon the Canadian Indians began to explore a route taken earlier by the tribes based in the United States.

Patterned after the Alaska organization, the Native Brotherhood of British Columbia was established in 1931. After an exhaustive study of the organization, historian Philip Drucker concluded that the group's success was in not achieving its early goals of acculturation of the Indian but in "bolstering the Indian's racial pride, though therefore defeating the aim of detribalizing him."[47]

Many other Indian organizations sprang up, but were not truly representative of the Indians as a whole. Even though they were factional groups, they made their voices heard. And still the land question remained.

The Land Question: A Final Agreement

Never far from the minds of the Nisga'a Tribal Council was the land issue, and in 1968 litigation was initiated in the British Columbia Supreme Court. Although the decision handed down five

Canadian Indian-rights advocate Jane Stewart. Stewart's reform program, Gathering Strength, is aimed at improving Indians' conditions.

During the 1990s, Canada, the British Columbia government, and the Nisga'a Tribal Council held some five hundred consultations and public information meetings. The Indians had an advocate in Jane Stewart, Minister of Indian Affairs and Northern Development, who called the Indian Act, "parochial, paternalistic and controlling."[48] The Indians did not even get the unrestricted right to vote until 1957, but things are changing, and Stewart's reform program, called Gathering Strength, is aimed at substantially altering the Indians' circumstances.

In May 1999, a final agreement was signed. The benefits to the fifty-five-hundred-member Nisga'a band are great: 769 square miles of land, $165.7 million, and powers of self-government in adoption, citizenship, and land management. The Nisga'a agree that this is a final settlement of their aboriginal rights.

This treaty will not be a pattern for settlements with other tribes, because each one will be treated individually to deal with specific circumstances. But this is a landmark agreement, paving the way for other long-awaited rights for the coastal Indians in Canada.

years later was vague, it recognized possible existence of aboriginal rights and prompted Canada to reassess the Indian Act and address the issue of aboriginal land claims.

Preserving the Past

The Indians of the Northwest Coast are using the court system to reclaim lost rights to their land, and they are turning to each other to reclaim lost pieces of their culture. Many Indians have a renewed interest in their arts, their crafts, and their sense of community. That sense of community was once assured by traditions including the longhouse, in which many families lived together in close quarters. The replacement of the longhouse with the single-family house has increased separation between members of the Northwest coastal tribes.

The loss of community, and a desire to somehow restore it, inspired Kwakiutl chief James Sewid and others in his band council in Alert Bay, British Columbia, to build a gathering place where members could meet and immerse themselves in their culture. The result was a longhouse that measures seventy feet by fifty feet. The house posts feature totems of Thunderbird and Grizzly Bear, crests from nearby tribes. The house front has a replica of a killer whale. This ceremonial building, which opened in 1966, is a place where the community comes together. The chief explained his interest:

> In the back of my mind one of the main reasons for building that community house was to have a place where we could try to preserve the art of my people. I knew it was going to be lost if we didn't try to pick it up and it wasn't just because the people were losing interest. The main reason that our customs, dances and art were dying out was that they had been forbidden by the law against our will. In fact, many of our people had been put in prison for refusing to give up our way of life.[49]

Other communities are also reexamining their culture. Indian artists are carving totem poles again, recording the history of their people. Although many poles have been copied from traditional designs, sev-

Today, many Indians have a renewed interest in the arts and other aspects of their culture.

in all its beauty and fury, when the people bowed to rain and storms in planning the day's work, has been replaced with alarm clocks and time clocks.

Western Europeans had millennia to make the gradual change from life in caves to a tribal existence to an agrarian economy to the industrial revolution. The coastal Indians have lived through only a few generations since contact with more "civilized" people introduced them to shame, disease, and alcohol, conveying as well the impression that native spirituality was somehow inferior. Is it a wonder that many of today's totem pole Indians have low self-esteem?

eral artists are developing their own style in this ancient art form. New poles are being raised in the ancient tradition, not just on museum grounds, but in communities.

The Indians who spotted explorer James Cook's ships barely two hundred years ago would not recognize their own descendants today. Gone are cedar-bark robes; today's jeans replace them. It is not just the trappings of society that have changed. Instead of processing the shredded bark for the robe and weaving it, now Native Americans work for wages to buy what they wear. The day-to-day existence with nature

By today's standards, many Native Americans live in poverty. School dropout rates exceed national norms in both the United States and Canada. Alcoholism is rampant. Suicide rates are staggering. Have there been too many demands of change in too short a time?

The difference in values between Western society and totem pole society is huge. Although both systems value accumulated wealth and the prestige associated with it, the great difference lies in standards for the appropriate display of affluence. In Western society, opulence is displayed in houses with grand lawns, new cars, and stock portfolios. In totem pole society, opulence is given away to prove that an inherited name, a privilege, and new rank are deserved.

When anthropologist Franz Boas asked permission of a Kwakiutl council to study their culture, he was told by a chief,

Do you see yon woods? Do you see yon trees? We shall cut them down and build new houses and live as our fathers did. We will dance when our laws command us to dance, we will feast when our hearts command us to feast. Do we ask the white man "Do as the Indian does"? No, we do not. Why then do you ask us "Do as the white man does"? It is a strict law that bids us dance. It is a strict law that bids us distribute our property among our friends and neighbors. It is a good law. Let the white man observe his law, we shall observe ours. And now if you are come to forbid us, begone, if not, you will be welcome to us.[50]

A resurgence of pride in their culture has prompted totem pole Indians to rediscover their past. A return to the spiritual philosophy of the Indian people and living in harmony with the land are the goals of many totem pole Indians. Of course, they cannot go back in time, nor would they want to. Today's Indian must choose what is good in today's society and incorporate it with what was good in the society in which his or her ancestors lived.

Notes

Chapter 1: The People and Their Land

1. Alvin M. Josephy Jr., *500 Nations.* New York: Alfred A. Knopf, 1994, p. 339.
2. Peter R. Gerber, *Indians of the Northwest Coast.* New York: Facts On File, 1989, pp. 85–86.
3. Philip Drucker, *Cultures of the North Pacific Coast.* San Francisco: Chandler Publishing, 1965, p. 122.
4. Drucker, *Cultures of the North Pacific Coast,* p. 49.
5. Quoted in Editors of Time-Life Books, *Keepers of the Totem.* Alexandria, VA: Time-Life Books, 1993, p. 45.

Chapter 2: Summer Harvest

6. Quoted in Norman Bancroft-Hunt, *People of the Totem: The Indians of the Pacific Northwest.* New York: G. P. Putnam's Sons, 1979, p. 72.
7. Quoted in Editors of Time-Life Books, *Keepers of the Totem,* p. 31.
8. Drucker, *Cultures of the North Pacific Coast,* p. 118.
9. Quoted in Editors of Time-Life Books, *Keepers of the Totem,* p. 39.
10. Editors of Time-Life Books, *Keepers of the Totem,* p. 84.
11. Quoted in Gerber, *Indians of the Northwest Coast,* p. 46.
12. Drucker, *Cultures of the North Pacific Coast,* p. 142.

Chapter 3: Life in Winter

13. Quoted in Bancroft-Hunt, *People of the Totem,* p. 28.
14. Joseph H. Wherry, *The Totem Pole Indians.* New York: Wilfred Funk, 1964, p. 31.
15. Quoted in Editors of Time-Life Books, *Keepers of the Totem,* p. 44.
16. Bancroft-Hunt, *People of the Totem,* p. 17.
17. Quoted in Editors of Time-Life Books, *Keepers of the Totem,* p. 77.

Chapter 4: Religion, Ceremonies, and Spirits

18. Editors of Time-Life Books, *Keepers of the Totem,* p. 85.
19. Editors of Time-Life Books, *Keepers of the Totem,* p. 85.
20. Quoted in Editors of Time-Life Books, *Keepers of the Totem,* p. 101.
21. Quoted in Editors of Time-Life Books, *Keepers of the Totem,* p. 106.
22. Drucker, *Cultures of the North Pacific Coast,* p. 88.
23. Quoted in Wherry, *The Totem Pole Indians,* p. 62.
24. Quoted in Bancroft-Hunt, *People of the Totem,* p. 110.

Chapter 5: The White Man Arrives

25. Quoted in Editors of Time-Life Books, *Keepers of the Totem,* p. 139.

26. Quoted in Bancroft-Hunt, *People of the Totem*, pp. 13–14.

27. Quoted in Bancroft-Hunt, *People of the Totem*, p. 14.

28. Quoted in George Woodcock, *Peoples of the Coast*. Bloomington: Indiana University Press, 1977, p. 11.

29. Quoted in Woodcock, *Peoples of the Coast*, p. 11.

30. Quoted in Woodcock, *Peoples of the Coast*, p. 112.

31. Quoted in Bancroft-Hunt, *People of the Totem*, p. 17.

32. Quoted in Editors of Time-Life Books, *Keepers of the Totem*, p. 154.

33. Quoted in Editors of Time-Life Books, *Keepers of the Totem*, p. 155.

34. Quoted in Editors of Time-Life Books, Keepers of the Totem, p. 158.

35. Quoted in Gerber, *Indians of the Northwest Coast*, p. 70.

36. Quoted in Woodcock, *Peoples of the Coast*, p. 203.

Chapter 6: Changing Cultures

37. Quoted in Drucker, *Cultures of the North Pacific Coast*, p. 207.

38. Drucker, *Cultures of the North Pacific Coast*, p. 217.

39. Quoted in Drucker, *Cultures of the North Pacific Coast*, p. 214.

40. Quoted in Editors of Time-Life Books, *Keepers of the Totem*, p. 169.

41. Quoted in H. R. Hays, *Children of the Raven: The Seven Indian Nations of the Northwest Coast*. New York: McGraw-Hill, 1975, p. 277.

42. Sealaska, Frequently Asked Questions, www.sealaska.com/html/FAQ.HTM, last modified December 1, 1999.

43. Quoted in Editors of Time-Life Books, *Keepers of the Totem*, p. 171.

44. Quoted in The Aboriginal Rights Coalition of British Columbia, Key Dates, www.arcbc.tripod.com/dates.htm, last updated December 28, 1999.

45. Quoted in Douglas Cole and Ira Chaikin, *An Iron Hand upon the People: The Law Against the Potlatch on the Northwest Coast*. Seattle: University of Washington Press, 1990, p. 15.

46. Quoted in Gerber, *Indians of the Northwest Coast*, p. 170.

47. Philip Drucker, *The Native Brotherhoods: Modern Intertribal Organizations on the Northwest Coast*. Washington, DC: Smithsonian Institution, 1958, p. 160.

48. Quoted in Andrew Purvis, "Whose Home and Native Land?" *Time*, February 15, 1999.

Conclusion: Preserving the Past

49. Quoted in Hays, *Children of the Raven*, p. 286.

50. Quoted in Hays, *Children of the Raven*, p. 88.

For Further Reading

Reg Ashwell, *Coast Salish: Their Art, Culture and Legends.* Blaine, WA: Hancock House, 1978. Ashwell interweaves the origins, culture, and folklore of the Salish in a readable volume.

Mary Giraudo Beck, *Shamans and Kushtakas: North Coast Tales of the Supernatural.* Seattle, WA: Alaska Northwest Books, 1991. The history and legends of the Tlingit and Haida are presented.

Don E. Beyer, *The Totem Pole Indians of the Northwest.* New York: Franklin Watts, 1989. Written on a third-grade level, this book gives an overall view of the totem pole Indians. It gives pictures and a good deal of information on the buried ruins in Washington.

Crisca Bierwert, *Brushed by Cedar, Living by the River: Coast Salish Figures of Power.* Tucson: University of Arizona Press, 1999. Through literary and social analysis, the author examines the importance of power, place, and longhouse ceremonies of the Coast Salish.

Cottie A. Burland, *North American Indian Mythology.* New York: Peter Bedrick Books, 1965. A former ethnographer with the British Museum, Burland's fascination for tribes of North America shines through in his well-researched volume. The spirit life of many Indian tribes is explored.

George F. MacDonald, *Haida Art.* Seattle: University of Washington Press, 1996. Nearly two hundred pictures and photographs of Haida art from the collection at the Canadian Museum of Civilization are presented within their historic and cultural setting.

Edward Malin, *Totem Poles of the Pacific Northwest Coast.* Portland, OR: Timber Press, 1994. The author presents the cultural, spiritual, and social traditions of the totem pole Indians. The text is illustrated with many line drawings and photographs.

James A. Maxwell, ed., *America's Fascinating Indian Heritage.* Pleasantville, NY: Reader's Digest, 1990. This updated volume includes recent developments in Native American culture and the resurgence of Indian art. It is organized regionally and chronologically and gives a balanced view of Native American customs and daily life.

Jay Miller, *Tsimshian Culture: A Light Through the Ages.* Lincoln: University of Nebraska Press, 1997. The author attributes the vitality of the Tsimshian to the way they capture light in their lives, from the legends of the beginning of light to the present day. Miller explains the cultural life of the Tsimshian around a metaphor of light.

Petra Press, *Indians of the Northwest: Traditions, History, Legends, and Life.* Philadelphia: Courage Books, 1997. This excellent book for younger readers shows why the culture of the Pacific Northwest Indians was so unique.

Works Consulted

Books

Norman Bancroft-Hunt, *People of the Totem: The Indians of the Pacific Northwest.* New York: G. P. Putnam's Sons, 1979. This book explores the art and ceremony of the totem pole Indians. Color photographs of artifacts add to the text.

Ruth Brindze, *The Story of the Totem Pole.* New York: Vanguard Press, 1951. The author recounts stories of feuds over the tallest totem pole, the European reaction to the poles, and the story behind the totem pole with Abraham Lincoln's likeness carved on it.

Frank Cassidy, ed., *Reaching Just Settlements.* Halifax, Nova Scotia: Institute for Research on Public Policy, 1991. The editor reprints speeches made at a conference on the aboriginal land question in February 1990.

Douglas Cole and Ira Chaikin, *An Iron Hand upon the People: The Law Against the Potlatch on the Northwest Coast.* Seattle: University of Washington Press, 1990. The authors describe the complex institution and present balanced accounts of the pros and cons of the law. The final chapter is titled "What Is Best for the Indians," and deals with how the government perceives this and how the authors view it as well.

Ross Cox, *The Columbia River.* Norman: University of Oklahoma Press, 1957. This diary of a trader gives a firsthand view of the Indian tribes who lived in Washington.

Philip Drucker, *Cultures of the North Pacific Coast.* San Francisco: Chandler Publishing, 1965. The author presents a clear picture of the Indians' way of life. Line drawings show how tools, fishing gear, and boxes were made.

———, *The Native Brotherhoods: Modern Intertribal Organizations on the Northwest Coast.* Washington, DC: Smithsonian Institution, 1958. The author visited Brotherhood meetings and gathered information on how these organizations have tried to solve Indian problems of acculturation.

Editors of Time-Life Books, *Keepers of the Totem*. Alexandria, VA: Time-Life Books, 1993. This well-researched volume includes extensive coverage of the religion of the Northwest Indians. The pictures of artifacts are extraordinary.

Peter R. Gerber, *Indians of the Northwest Coast*. New York: Facts On File, 1989. Striking photographs illustrate this volume. The author details the troubled relationship between the early European explorers and traders and the Indians.

Robert Steven Grumet, *Native Americans of the Northwest Coast: A Critical Bibliography*. Bloomington: Indiana University Press, 1979. This book, which introduces the culture of the Pacific Northwest Coast Indians, gives a scholarly analysis of the major works about the area and its people.

Erna Gunther, *Indian Life on the Northwest Coast of North America*. Chicago: University of Chicago Press, 1972. This book quotes eyewitness accounts of the Indians by explorers of the last decades of the eighteenth century.

H. R. Hays, *Children of the Raven: The Seven Indian Nations of the Northwest Coast*. New York: McGraw-Hill, 1975. The author traces the Indians' history from the time of their encounters with white people. He interviewed Indians during his trip through this area and conveys their feelings toward acculturation.

Diane Hoyt-Goldsmith, *Totem Pole*. New York: Holiday House, 1990. This book follows a modern Tsimshian Indian as he carves a totem pole for a neighboring tribe. Steps from choosing the straight cedar tree to erecting the finished totem pole are explained and enhanced with photos.

Alvin M. Josephy Jr., *500 Nations*. New York: Alfred A. Knopf, 1994. This hefty volume by a distinguished scholar explores Native American history and culture. Different nations and tribes are profiled with maps, illustrations, and photographs supplementing the text.

Emerson N. Matson, *Longhouse Legends*. Nashville, TN: Thomas Nelson and Sons, 1968. This volume recounts legends told by the

Indians who lived around Puget Sound. Some were chanted as the Indians danced.

James A. Maxwell, ed., *America's Fascinating Indian Heritage.* Pleasantville, NY: Reader's Digest, 1978. This book divides the Indian tribes into regions and carefully details how the various regions dictated the lifestyle of the Indians. Sidebars and a multitude of photos and illustrations show the customs of the various tribes.

Gary E. Moulton, ed., *The Journals of the Lewis and Clark Expedition.* Vol. 10. Lincoln: University of Nebraska Press, 1996. This volume presents the journal of Sergeant Patrick Gass, May 14, 1804–September 23, 1806, with an emphasis on daily details. Includes footnotes to explain exactly where the expedition was in terms of present-day towns and counties.

Robert H. Ruby and John A. Brown, *Indians of the Pacific Northwest.* Norman: University of Oklahoma Press, 1981. This book chronicles Indian-white relations throughout the entire Northwest.

Bonnie Shemie, *Houses of Wood.* New York: Tundra Books, 1992. This book shows how prehistoric Pacific Northwest Indians built their frame houses and made their plank boards with the use of simple tools such as an adze, an ax, and wedges.

Hilary Stewart, *Artifacts of the Northwest Coast Indians.* Saanichton, British Columbia: Hancock House, 1973. Pictures and drawings of artifacts, where they were found, and which tribe used them form the basis for the study.

———, *Totem Poles.* Seattle: University of Washington Press, 1990. The author presents an historical overview of totem poles and details the crests, carved figures, and how poles are carved.

William C. Sturtevant, *Boxes and Bowls.* Washington, DC: Smithsonian Institution Press, 1973. This book on a unique aspect of totem pole culture was published concurrently with an exhibit at the Smithsonian Institution.

Joseph H. Wherry, *The Totem Pole Indians.* New York: Wilfred Funk, 1964. This volume tells of the origin of the Totemland Indians, their encounters with explorers and where totem poles are on permanent display in museums in the United States, Canada, and Europe.

George Woodcock, *Peoples of the Coast*. Bloomington: Indiana University Press, 1977. This volume focuses on the beginnings of the migrations to the Northwest Coast and the spiritual side of the Indians.

Periodical

Andrew Purvis, "Whose Home and Native Land?" *Time,* February 15, 1999.

Websites

The Aboriginal Rights Coalition of British Columbia (arcbc. tripod.com). The Aboriginal Rights Coalition of British Columbia is committed to justice for the First Nations. The website presents history of the First Nations, facts about the land question, events of interest, and treaty progress.

Sealaska Corporation (www.sealaska.com). The Sealaska Corporation is owned by the Haida and Tlingit who live in Alaska. The website covers the company's history, news, and other timely information about the company.

Index

afterlife, 46–47

Alaska
  influence of missionaries in, 70–71
  military rule in, 69–70
  status of Native Americans in, 73–75
  U.S. government purchases, 69–70
  white settlement of, 71–72

Alaska Native Brotherhood, 73

Alaska Native Claims Settlement Act (1971), 74

Animal People, 36

animal spirits, 48–49

artifacts, 7–8

artwork, 7–8

baskets, 39

bears, 14, 48–49

Bering, Vitus, 58

Beringia, 12

berry picking, 26–27

blankets, 63–64

Blenkinsop, George, 76

Boas, Franz, 7, 24–25

boxes, 11, 38–39

British Columbia
  land question in, 77–79
  Native Americans in, 75–79
  potlatch ban in, 76–77

Canada
  history of Native Americans in, 75–79
  land claims in, 77–79

candlefish, 23

canoes, 11, 15, 62

celebrations. *See* potlatches

ceremonies
  dancing societies and, 56–57
  for spirits, 55–56

chiefs, 17–18
  validation of, 42, 44–45

children
  apprenticeship of, 52
  naming of, 17
  spirit quests by, 49–52

Chinook jargon, 61

Christianity, 65–68

citizenship, 73

clan ties, 18

climate, 10–11

clothing, 24

Coast Salish, 14, 69
  Spirit Singing of, 55–56

commoners, 18–19

Cook, James (Captain), 59–60

cooking methods, 38–39

Cranmer, Daniel (chief), 76

culture
  renewed interest in Native American, 80–81

Cultures of the North Pacific Coast (Drucker), 30

dances, 51

dancing societies, 56–57

Davis, Jeff C., 69–70

death, 46–47

dentalia shells, 32, 33

disease, 64

dogs, 28

Douglas, James, 65

Drucker, Philip, 26
  description of whale hunting by, 30, 32
  on missionaries, 70–71
  on shamans, 53
  on social order, 19

Duncan, William, 66–68

Picture Credits

About the Author

Veda Boyd Jones enjoys the challenge of writing for diverse readers. She is the author of twenty-four books: four children's historical novels, seven children's biographies, two children's nonfiction books, a picture book, nine romance novels, and a coloring book. Other published works include over 150 articles and stories in magazines such as *Cricket, Highlights, Humpty Dumpty, The Writer, Writer's Digest,* and *Woman's World,* and articles in reference books. Jones earned an M.A. in history at the University of Arkansas, has taught writing at Crowder College in Neosho, Missouri, and currently teaches for the Institute of Children's Literature. She and her husband, Jimmie, have three sons, Landon, Morgan, and Marshall.